WILLIAMS-SONOMA

ESSENTIALS OF French COOKING

GENERAL EDITOR
CHUCK WILLIAMS

PHOTOGRAPHY
TUCKER & HOSSLER

RECIPES
GEORGEANNE BRENNAN

TEXT
SARAH PUTMAN CLEGG

Oxmoor House®

Contents

When I made my first trip to Paris in 1973, little did I know that France in general and French food in particular would forever become the focus of my life. I may hold an American passport, but somewhere in my soul, there is surely a strong French connection.

What is it about French food that draws us in and warms our spirits? Much of it has to do with tradition. So much of the pleasure of life and of food is drawn from memories: our grandmother's pie, a special aunt's potato salad, our mother's golden homemade rolls. I did not grow up eating French food, but once it was put before me as an adult, I instantly understood that tradition and excellence pay off in a big way. No matter our culinary background, we instinctively swoon over the perfect upside-down apple tart known as *tarte tatin*; fragrant cheese puffs, or *gougères,* warm from the oven; the soothing winter combination of duck and white beans called cassoulet; and the ever-popular classic lemon pie, *tarte au citron.*

I have lived permanently in France since 1980, and with each day I discover something different about an ingredient, learn an interesting tidbit of French food history, or find joy in the sighting of a new cheese or a new bread, or the sampling of a new wine. The excitement never wears off. As I explore the outdoor markets daily, I'm happy to spot the first-of-season spring asparagus or France's first crop of golden lemons from the town of Menton, near Nice. My own summer garden in Provence allows me to make the freshest ratatouille and the most stunning vegetable *soupe au pistou.* The orchards offer a bounty of cherries for a late-spring cherry clafouti, and the winter soil yields fresh black truffles for flavoring a serving of creamy scrambled eggs.

Recipes for all these, and more, can be found within these pages. So now it is your turn: don an apron, roll up your sleeves, light the oven, take out the sauté pan, and delve into the marvelous collection of traditional French recipes offered here. To all, a hearty bon appétit!

Patricia Wells

The Influence of French Cuisine

France has long enjoyed a reputation as the originator of the world's greatest cuisine. Whether or not the rest of the world agrees, the French certainly believe it. This book gives an overview of the rich culinary traditions of France, so that you can bring its essential dishes to your own table.

The approach to cooking as an art form goes back centuries in France. Blessed with a varied geography and a wealth of natural resources, a long coastline and plenty of fertile farmland, France was eagerly colonized by the Romans beginning in the first century AD. The Romans brought with them favored ingredients and a certain taste for luxury: they planted vineyards in Burgundy and Bordeaux, imported plump snails to feed on the grape leaves, and even introduced a rudimentary form of foie gras, or fattened goose or duck liver, which is so emblematic of high-end French cuisine today.

Centuries later, after throwing off the Roman yoke and absorbing an onslaught of invaders, the French kings, Burgundian dukes, and counts of Toulouse emerged from the Dark Ages immensely powerful and wealthy. They famously indulged in an elaborate tradition of banquets featuring all manner of game, sweet and spiced specialties, and edible sculptures.

SOPHISTICATION AND SIMPLICITY

The type of complex food that the words *French cuisine* still evoke—those dishes napped in rich cream sauces and garnished with caviar, foie gras, truffles, or gold leaf, those that demand several days and a team of trained cooks to create—was a creation of chefs to the rich and noble in the regions surrounding Paris, Île-de-France, and the Loire Valley. This highly stylized form of cooking, called *haute cuisine*, "high cooking," evolved in turn out of the common cooking style of the region, known in France as *cuisine bourgeoise*, perhaps best translated as "skillful home cooking." The regional dishes of Île-de-France, such as coq au vin and veal *blanquette*, may seem generically French, until you learn that these dishes were originally preparations based on local ingredients and that over time they came to define the cuisine of the country as a whole.

The names of influential chefs of centuries past are familiar names in France and to aficionados of French cuisine outside the country. Taillevent, chef to Charles V, reigned in medieval times. La Varenne helped codify and simplify French cooking in the seventeenth century, and Paul Bocuse distilled it into nouvelle cuisine in the 1970s. But there is another side to French cuisine, the *cuisine du terroir*, "cooking of the land," which is indelibly tied to a specific place and to its particular native ingredients.

THE ROLE OF REGIONALITY

The vast French landscape is wonderfully diverse. The country was historically divided into provinces that were transformed into "regions" after the French Revolution in the late 1700s. Each province had its own distinct geography, with culinary specialties based on local resources. These local specialties might be raw ingredients, or they might be finished dishes, but in every case they were carefully cultivated or developed and perfected over the course of many centuries.

France has long been an inspiration for, and a leading influence on many of the world's finest cuisines.

The cheeses of France are known throughout the world. Nearly every region proudly makes its own variety.

Inaccessible mountain areas, for example, often came to specialize in aged goat's or sheep's milk cheeses as a way of preserving the milk of livestock in preparation for the harsh winter. On the Atlantic and north coasts, farming mussels and oysters on wooden stakes was found to slow the growth of the shellfish and produce the tiny, sweet specimens that are now coveted all over France. The average food-obsessed French person can tell you exactly which areas produce the best examples of each item, from artichokes and duck pâtés to madeleines and cherry eau-de-vie.

DEEP CULINARY ROOTS

Just as Parisian cuisine came to dominate French food culture, for centuries Paris itself overshadowed every other town as the dominant city in France, drawing the more ambitious sons and daughters from every outlying province. These immigrants came in droves but never forgot their home regions and their culinary specialties, and today Parisians whose families have lived in the city for centuries will tell you which *pays*, or rural area, their family members came. Their ancestral region is an integral part of their identity, and even French city dwellers possess an uncommon affinity for the land.

No matter where they settle, the French remember the rhythm of seasons in their cooking and eating, and demand nothing but the best quality in their raw ingredients. The idea of *terroir*, the unique and ineffable quality that food and wine derive from the soil, air, and other physical aspects of the environment in which it is created, is essential to French cooking. The true genius of French cuisine lies in its close ties to the land and its indigenous ingredients: the cheese caves of Roquefort; the mushroom caves of the Loire; the wild herbs of Haute-Provence that give savor to the flesh of game birds; the salt-sprayed coastal meadows of Normandy and Brittany that flavor the milk and meat of sheep and cattle; the oaks of the Périgord at whose bases black truffles grow; and the chestnut trees of Corsica that supply meal for porridge and flour for cakes. Although urban haute cuisine and nouvelle cuisine have wielded great influence in kitchens far beyond France's borders, the often simple and beloved homey regional specialties are what the French call *la vraie cuisine*, "the true cooking."

DAILY BREAD

A French meal is not typically the multi-course marathon that unfolds in top-shelf restaurants on special occasions, but it is, by some standards, an extended affair. Lunch is the most important meal of the day, and even French schoolchildren pause each morning on the way to class to inspect the school lunch menu du jour. Lunch break is usually about two hours, with families leaving work or school and returning home for the meal in smaller towns and villages. In the south of France, the two-hour break might extend into a full Mediterranean-style siesta. A big Sunday lunch with the extended family is not unusual.

Dinner will usually be a lighter but similarly leisurely meal, and breakfast is often nothing more than a pastry and a coffee. Wine is generally enjoyed with both lunch and dinner. Bread is always offered at a French meal, and cheese is commonly enjoyed as a separate course before dessert. Every region of France lists among its specialties certain wines and cheeses, both of which make excellent complements to the typical ingredients and dishes of the area.

ANGLETERRE

MANCHE

• Rouen

NORMANDIE

BELGIQUE

NORD –
PAS DE
CALAIS

PICARDIE

ALLEMAGNE

LUXEMBOURG

CHAMPAGNE-
ARDENNE

LORRAINE

BRETAGNE

Paris
ÎLE-DE-
FRANCE

• Strasbourg
ALSACE

PAYS-DE-
LA-LOIRE

FRANCE

• Tours
CENTRE

Dijon •
BOURGOGNE

FRANCHE-
COMTÉ

SUISSE

POITOU-
CHARENTES
Cognac
•

• Limousin

• Lyon
RHÔNE-ALPES

OCÉAN
ATLANTIQUE

AUVERGNE

ITALIE

• Bordeaux
AQUITAINE

MIDI-PYRÉNÉES
Toulouse •

PROVENCE
Nice •
• Marseille
•

MONACO

LANGUEDOC-
ROUSSILLON

CORSE

ANDORRE

ESPAGNE

MER MÉDITERRANÉE

0 KM   100   200
0 MI   100   200

The Regions

Since the French Revolution, mainland France has been divided into 21 regions, plus the island of Corsica. Some modern-day regions correspond to historical provinces; others are more contemporary creations. Each has its own distinct geography, culture, and culinary specialties.

ALSACE

Sausages and Sauerkraut

If you want to eat great German food in France, go to Alsace. This easternmost region shares a border as well as one of the most famous rivers with Germany, the Rhine. Culturally and gastronomically, Alsace has more in common with Germany than with the rest of France. The capital, Strasbourg, is known for its beer, but Alsace is also one of the most important wine regions in France, producing mainly light and refreshing whites. These are not used extensively in cooking, but provide a welcome counterpoint to the hearty, rich fare. Pork and goose are favored meats in Alsace, and their fats are traditionally used for cooking. The region is known and admired for its pork products, and Alsatian pork sausage is second to none. Most geese in Alsace are destined for foie gras. Along with the Périgord, Alsace is a top producer of foie gras, but neither can claim to have invented it—that honor goes to the ancient Egyptians, who then passed the technique on to the Romans, who brought a taste for it to France.

Culinary Signature: Choucroute

Unlike many other regions of France, Alsace does not have a dominant native ingredient that distinguishes it from its neighbors. However, it has one particular dish that stands out: choucroute, or sauerkraut. When you see the term *à l'alsacienne* (Alsatian style) on a menu in France, you can bet that the dish you're ordering will be accompanied by choucroute. To prepare it, cabbage is pickled in an earthenware jar for several weeks, fermenting in its own juices and in a blend of aromatics such as onion, juniper berries, cloves, and bay leaves. *Choucroute garnie*, "garnished sauerkraut," may include different types of sausages, bacon, smoked ham, smoked goose, and even partridge, in any combination or all together.

Regional Specialties

Foie gras Livers of geese that are enlarged by fattening up the birds on noodles or corn for three weeks before slaughter

Saucisse de Strasbourg Pork sausage similar to German knockwurst, made of pork and beef and lightly smoked

Apätzli Curly handmade noodles

Oie à l'alsacienne Alsatian-style goose stuffed with sausages and roasted

Bäckeofe A baked dish of beef, pork, and lamb or mutton with onions and potatoes

Flammeküche Quiche with onions, bacon, and crème fraîche, also known as *tarte flambée*

Vol-au-vent In Alsace, this popular savory pastry is often stuffed with chicken

Tarte à l'alsacienne Fruit tarts, especially apple and plum, with custard or cream

AQUITAINE

The Richest Tapestry

The region of Aquitaine in southwest France is one of excellent food and great culinary contrasts. Its capital, Bordeaux, is situated in one of the best wine-making areas in the world, rivaled in France only by Burgundy. Bordeaux's refined cooking style is a thoroughly urban one, cultivated over centuries in this wealthy port city, which was for many years a holding of the English, thanks to the marriage of Eleanor of Aquitaine to England's Henry II. To the south and southeast of Bordeaux lie Gascony and the Dordogne, home of the truffle and a center of foie gras production, where peasant cuisine is exalted. These areas are supported by a naturally rich and fertile landscape producing excellent fruits and vegetables and armies of ducks and geese. In the far southwest rises the nearly insurmountable range of the Pyrenees, home of the Basques, whose language and origins are a mystery and whose cooking style shares more with the Spanish Basques on the Southern side of the mountains than with their immediate French neighbors.

Culinary Signature: Truffles

The prized and pricey black truffle grows at the foot of oak trees in the Périgord and in Gascony, where foragers seek it out in autumn and winter. The white truffles of Italy's Piedmont region are scarcer and thus more expensive, but the black ones have a more robust flavor. Whether black or white, truffles are one of the most expensive foodstuffs on earth, pound per pound. Truffle lovers by nature, pigs were traditionally used to root them out, but many truffles were lost to the pigs by this method. Dogs are now preferred, as they can be trained to find the fungus and relied upon to relinquish it without a fight. In these areas, truffles are used to enhance every possible dish, from refined sauces and terrines of foie gras to scrambled eggs. The menu term *à la périgordine* means that a dish includes shaved truffles and sometimes foie gras.

Regional Specialties

Foie gras As in Alsace, enlarged goose liver is a specialty here, served with grapes from the vineyards

Confit Salted goose and duck legs slowly braised in their own fat

Cèpes Porcini mushrooms that are foraged in the region

Walnut oil An important crop in the southwest; their oil gives delicious flavor to salad dressings and cakes

Agen prunes Brought to Agen by the Romans, these famous fruits now enjoy AOC status (page 31)

Bayonne ham Air-cured ham from the gastronomic capital of Basque country, produced from pigs that feast on chestnuts, acorns, and roots

Oysters The briny oysters of Arcachon on the Atlantic coast are widely admired

Lamb The salt-sprayed pastures that border the west coast give superb flavor to the lambs that graze on them

Canelès, mini caramel cakes, acquire their unique shape from being baked in special copper molds.

Ortolans Small songbirds considered a delicacy when fattened up, drowned in Armagnac, spit-roasted, and devoured bones and all

Garbure Gascon country soup featuring seasonal vegetables and sometimes ham, salt pork, or goose confit

Pipérade Basque dish combining scrambled eggs with sautéed onions, tomatoes, and the mildly piquant pepper named *piment d'Espellete*, enjoyed at any time of day

Sauce bordelaise Decadently rich sauce for beef that combines red Bordeaux wine, butter, tomato, and marrow

Canelés de Bordeaux Small cylindrical cakes with a dark brown, crunchy exterior that conceals a light, custardy center

Chocolate When chocolate was first introduced to France, Bayonne was the only city that produced it, and it remains a specialty there to this day

Sauternes Luscious, golden white dessert wine, a natural match with foie gras

Armagnac One of France's two great grape brandies, Armagnac hails from Gascony

Eaux-de-vie Aquitaine produces a number of fruit brandies, especially those made from currants, quinces, and walnuts

AUVERGNE

Desolate Grandeur

The Auvergne is a remote, rugged region of France, part of the volcanic mountain range in the south-central part of the country known as the Massif Central. The passage of ancient glaciers here created a striking landscape, dotted with hot springs. The climate is harsh, with hot summers and very cold winters, and the Auvergnats are known for their toughness. As befits a hardy mountain people, the region's traditional cuisine is simple and satisfying,

The town of Le Puy is famous for its green lentils, which have AOC designation.

depending on honest and humble ingredients like potatoes, cabbage, and cheese, plus excellent pork and mutton raised on mountain pastures. The Auvergne is cattle country as well and hence the birthplace of several notable cow's milk cheeses.

Culinary Signature: Le Puy Lentils

The volcanic soil around Le Puy, a medieval hill town in the Haute-Loire area, is perfect for growing lentils. Tiny green lentils are grown here without fertilizer and enjoy protected AOC status (page 31). They have a robust, earthy flavor and maintain a firm texture after they are cooked.

Regional Specialties

Morilles Earthy morel mushrooms grow wild and are foraged in the forests of Auvergne

Saucisse sèche d'Auvergne The local dry pork sausage, aged for two months

Aligot This characteristic dish combines mashed potatoes with light *tomme* cheese, a type made from skim milk, and sometimes garlic, and is eaten with sausages

Cabbage soup Cabbage and salt pork cooked in an earthenware pot form the basis of two traditional Auvergnat dishes: *soupe aux choux*, or cabbage soup, and *potée auvergnate*

Tripoux Braised packets of veal and mutton tripe filled with herbs and vegetables

BRITTANY (BRETAGNE)

Celtic France

The remote northwestern region of France that juts out into the English Channel, Brittany historically has more in common with Britain than with the rest of France and tends to set itself apart. Its population is mostly descended from Celts who fled across the channel from Britain during the Anglo-Saxon conquest, and even today its indigenous language, Breton, and Welsh are mutually spoken. Brittany has always been a poor region, where the peasantry eked out a hardscrabble existence from farming and fishing, and many women were perpetually dressed in mourning for husbands and sons

Savory crêpes, with nutty buckwheat flour, are a Breton tradition.

lost at sea. The cuisine is based on simple ingredients and featuring many types of fish and seafood.

Culinary Signature: Crêpes

Made from buckwheat for a savory version and regular flour for a sweet one, the crêpe is Brittany's most distinctive dish. Savory crêpes, called galettes, are thin, wide, and sturdy, and usually contain meat, fish, or cheese, or a combination. One of the most popular galettes at *crêperies* in Brittany and throughout France is the *complète*, combining ham, egg, and cheese. Local Breton ingredients, such as apples and cream or salted butter caramel, make simple and delectable fillings for dessert crêpes.

Regional Specialties

Fleur de sel This gray sea salt is harvested by hand off the Brittany coast and in salt marshes, most notably in Guérande and Noirmoutier

Cream and butter The native cattle breeds of Brittany give milk that is especially rich in cream and makes a lovely golden-hued butter

White beans The term *à la bretonne* on a menu indicates that a dish includes humble white beans, the most classic example being Breton-style roast leg of lamb with white beans

Oysters A number of varieties of both wild and cultivated oysters are harvested off the Breton coast and are typically enjoyed raw

Lobster The characteristic pot-au-feu, or peasant-style stew, of Brittany features lobster and an assortment of other shellfish

Lamb The lamb and mutton of Brittany are admired for the salt flavor that imbues them as sheep graze on sea-sprayed meadows

Cotriade The Breton version of bouillabaisse, this fish stew contains several kinds of fish and potatoes, but no shellfish

Kouign amann Breton butter cake made from alternating layers of brioche dough with plenty of butter and sugar

Breton far A floury prune flan that is usually flavored with brandy, made in both savory and sweet versions

La cidrae Hard apple cider is the most popular beverage in Brittany, thanks to a chilly northern climate that favors apples

Couchen Type of mead, or honey wine, popular in Brittany

BURGUNDY (BOURGOGNE)

Magnificent Countryside

Along with Bordeaux, Burgundy is one of the two most important wine-producing regions in France and, it's fair to say, the world. As is usually the case in wine country, its food is top-notch as well. Burgundy enjoys great natural advantages and an illustrious history. The Grand Dukes of Burgundy, based in the city of Dijon, were once on par in strength and importance with the king of France, and married into or conquered territories of their own beyond France's borders. The Burgundians were wealthy and obsessed with good food, and their tables groaned under the weight of their legendary feasts. The development of gastronomy and viticulture in Burgundy was also influenced by a centuries-long struggle for political dominance between two powerful orders of medieval monks, the Benedictines, who were master winemakers based at the monastery of Cluny, and the Cistercians, who were the great farmers of their day and used at the monastery of Cîteaux.

Culinary Signature: Dijon Mustard

The mustard-loving Romans brought the mustard plant with them when they conquered Gaul. Although many mustards are made with vinegar, Dijon-style mustard carries on the ancient Roman tradition of using *verjus*, the juice of unripe green grapes. *Verjus* contributes

Gougéres, a popular hors d'oeuvre, are piped onto a baking sheet and then baked.

Gougères Savory bite-size pastries made of *choux* pastry and Gruyère cheese

Pain d'épices Lesser-known specialty of Dijon containing a delicious blend of warm spices; sometimes translated as gingerbread, it is more accurately "spice bread"

Crème de cassis Black currant liqueur, mixed with white wine or Champagne to make Kir or Kir Royal, two refreshing apéritifs named after a mayor of Dijon

CENTRE

The Garden of France

One of the earliest-settled areas of France, this modern region, which includes the historic provinces of Touraine (and its capital, Tours), Orléanais (and its capital, Orléans), and Berry (of the famous dukes), was once of greater political importance than Paris. Located here is the Val de Loire, the fertile valley where the Loire River winds past lush vineyards and magnificent châteaux, the country homes of French kings and nobles. The cuisine of Centre, like that of Île-de-France, may seem generically French and lacking any distinctive regional character until you realize that the local cuisine became the national cuisine and eventually imported abroad as French cooking.

The area is called the "garden of France," thanks to the abundance of fruits and vegetables that grow so well here. Also bountiful are game and fish. Historically the Sologne forest was the source of game that graced the tables of the French royalty, and hunting is still a flourishing pastime in Centre today. Small freshwater fish from the Loire might be fried whole for *friture de la Loire* and enjoyed with one of the excellent local white wines. Salmon, pike, carp, and perch are also caught here and often cooked in a white wine

a less acidic, subtler tang to mustard than vinegar does. The availability of grape juice was one factor that made Dijon, with its proximity to the great vineyards of Burgundy, a natural center of production for mustard as well. Mustard is an excellent accompaniment to beef, and it so happens that Burgundy beef is considered the best in France.

Regional Specialties

Escargots de Bourgogne The fat, black, luscious snails of Burgundy are widely acknowledged to be the best in France

Beef Burgundy is famous for the quality of its beef, the best of which comes from the local breed of Charolais cattle

Boeuf bourguignon Well-known beef stew made with red Burgundy wine, mushrooms, tiny onions, and bacon

Oeufs en meurette Poached eggs in red wine sauce, garnished with mushrooms, tiny onions, and *lardons*, small strips of pork fat

Cream sauces A natural culinary development in cattle-raising areas; to be paired with the prized beef of the region

Fresh seasonal vegetables are a necessary component of menus throughout the country.

(broad) beans, at their best when young and tender in the early spring, and light, fresh greens such as sorrel.

Centre is not only France's garden but also its orchard, known for tree fruits such as pears, apples, and plums. Roast pork with dried plums or cooked apples, a sweet and savory pairing of meat and fruit, is slightly unusual in traditional French cooking but is a natural in this fruit-growing region.

Regional Specialties

Mushrooms The majority of France's mushrooms are grown in the Loire Valley, in amazing mushroom caves located around the city of Saumur

Fougasse This artisanal bread often made into shapes—the most common being a stalk of wheat—is baked in ashes and derives its name from *focus*, the Roman word for "hearth"

Charcuterie Each town has its own specialties, but among the most admired are the rillettes de Tours, a potted pork spread, and the partridge pâté of Chartres

Andouillette The area around the commune of Vouvray is known for this tripe sausage, customarily cooked in the famous white Vouvray wine

Boudin blanc Soft white sausage made with veal, chicken, and sometimes sweetbreads; *boudin noir*, "black" or blood sausage, is made with pork and pig's blood

sauce. Another very typical specialty is goat cheese, often baked and placed still warm on freshly dressed greens and paired with Sancerre, a white wine.

Culinary Signature: Spring Vegetables and Orchard Fruits

Inscribed with the checkerboard patterns of farms, the rolling green hills of the Loire Valley have always been the picturesque heart of France. If the list of vegetables in which this area specializes also forms a list of the best produce of spring, perhaps it's because they all pair so nicely with the region's crisp white wines, made from Sauvignon Blanc and Chenin Blanc grapes. Some of the best asparagus in the world, kept white by depriving the plants of light, is grown in the sandy soil along the banks of the Loire. Artichokes, and their cousins, cardoons, are also grown here. They are thought to be two of the many culinary delights popularized by Catherine de Médici in the 1530s when she arrived from Italy with her retinue of chefs to marry Henri II. Other typical vegetables of the area are peas and fava

Spring peas are a sign of the changing season in both the kitchen gardens and markets of France.

Coq au vin The quintessential French dish of chicken braised in red wine comes from the Loire Valley

Matelot Red wine stew made with eel and very popular here as elsewhere in France

Pourlècheries The name of these stylized pastries, "things for licking," perfectly evokes the image of a child eating a sweet

Tarte tatin The famous upside-down caramelized apple tart is supposed to have originated here

Pithiviers Puff-pastry tart filled with frangipane and named for its town of origin, also famous for lark pâté

Beets, a main crop of Champagne-Ardenne, are the perfect accompaniment to fresh greens.

CHAMPAGNE-ARDENNE

Deep Forests and Dazzling Wines

Champagne-Ardenne is an exception to the usual rule that great wine-making areas tend to develop a great gastronomy alongside. Perhaps the challenge stems from the wine itself: Champagne is notoriously difficult to pair successfully with food, and cooking with Champagne wastes the sparkle that the winemakers have labored to add. Furthermore, although the land here makes good pastureland and is perfect for growing the grapes used in Champagne production—Chardonnay, Pinot Noir, and Meunier—it is not especially good farmland. The main crops of the region are humble and northern European in character: cabbage, beets, and barley. Whatever the reason, the cuisine of Champagne consists mostly of borrowings from neighboring Bourgogne, Alsace-Lorraine, and Île-de-France. However, its effervescent contribution to the French wine pantheon has earned the world's eternal gratitude.

Culinary Signature: Champagne

The Romans planted, or supplemented, grapevines in some of France's great wine-making areas to provide wine for their soldiers, in Burgundy and Bordeaux. But in the first century they began tearing out vines in certain other regions, fearing competition from French wines. This is often said to have been the case in Champagne, although scholars disagree on when vines were first planted there. In any case, the interruption did not last long, and wine has certainly been made in Champagne since the early fifth century. Until the seventeenth century, only regular wine was produced; the method of creating bubbles through fermentation in the bottle, a process called *méthode champenoise*, was discovered in the mid-1600s and refined by the monk Dom Perignon at the Abbey of Hautvillers.

Just a few dishes are made with Champagne wine: for example, it is used in the region to make a sauce for chicken or fish. Many believe that Champagne is best drunk unaccompanied as an appetizer or postprandial wine or, of course, as a celebratory beverage. Others say that its flavor is neutral enough that it can be served with dinner, though they acknowledge that it perhaps won't complement many foods as well as another wine would. Yet everyone agrees that Champagne pairs beautifully with oysters on the half shell.

The chestnut tree has thrived on the island of Corsica for centuries.

Regional Specialties

Game The deep forests of the Ardennes are notable for their game, and thrush and wild boar are used for local pâtés

Andouillette de Troyes Tripe sausage is made in many areas of France, but the one from the town of Troyes is especially well regarded

Pig's trotters Specialty of Sainte-Ménehould, where they are braised until tender, then rolled in bread crumbs and grilled until golden

Gougères de l'Aube These savory pastry tidbits, flavored with cheese, are enjoyed in the Aube but are actually a recipe borrowed from neighboring Burgundy

Eaux-de-vie Kirsch, brandy distilled from cherries, and *prunelle* from plums, both imports from Alsace and Lorraine, are made in the Champagne region

Marc de Champagne The leftovers from the first pressing of grapes for Champagne are fermented and distilled to produce this brandy

Ratafia A sweet local cordial made by blending unfiltered, unfermented grape juice with marc de Champagne and aging it for up to two years

CORSICA (CORSE)

The Island of Beauty

An island in the Mediterranean sea, Corsica lies closer to Italy than to mainland France. Since prehistoric times, it has been overrun by a long list of invaders, but today the inhabitants are mainly of Italian descent. The indigenous language is similar to Italian, and the food is more Italian than French. However, as the birthplace of Napoléon Bonaparte, Corsica remains eternally linked to France, and its scrubby moorlands, *les maquis*, are famous in France for providing a hideout not only for generations of bandits but for French resistance fighters of the Second World War. For an island cuisine, the food of Corsica is surprisingly meaty and lacking in seafood. The moorlands and mountains offer good pastureland for sheep and goats, whose milk goes into several local cheeses and excellent charcuterie selections are made from both wild boar and domestic pig.

Culinary Signature: Chestnuts

Wheat was once grown on Corsica, but the Italians demanded so much of it as tax payments that the Corsicans eventually gave up cultivating it and turned to chestnuts as their main source of flour. Corsica's ancient chestnut forests offer some of France's best. The nuts provide flour that goes into both sweet and savory dishes, and is combined with goat's milk to make a traditional soup, *minestra di castagnigna*. Chestnuts are also fed to pigs that are used to make *prizzutu*, an air-cured ham similar to prosciutto, which has a nutty flavor.

Regional Specialties

Pulenta Sweet chestnut-flour preparation that is similar to polenta

Capone Spit-roasted eels caught from the coastal wetlands

Figatelli Sausages produced from pork liver

Dziminu Spicy bouillabaisse-like fish stew

Minestra Hearty soup of beans, cabbage, potatoes, and smoked ham

Honey Corsican honey is the only French honey to bear the AOC designation (page 31)

Cedrat Local citrus fruit that tastes like a sweet lemon, used in desserts and made into an eau-de-vie

FRANCHE-COMTÉ

Fertile Lowlands and Mountain Fare

This lesser-known region of France, whose name means "free county (of Burgundy)," is sandwiched between Burgundy on the west and the country of Switzerland on the east. It includes the Jura mountain range and presents an interesting intersection of cuisine, where typically rustic mountain food meets the sophisticated Burgundy-influenced cooking of the lowlands. The Alpine soil of the Juras is poor, but the pasturage is excellent, and this, combined with the historical difficulty of transporting milk from the mountain areas, has made cheese production a specialty of the region. Mountain streams and forests provide plentiful freshwater fish such as salmon, game, and mushrooms for foraging. The wines produced in the Franche-Comté are hardly known outside of France, but are some of the most unique and interesting in the country and gaining in popularity throughout the world.

Culinary Signature: Comté

The cows that graze on the Alpine pastures of the Jura Mountains give milk that makes particularly fine cheese. The most beloved cheese of this region is Comté, also known as Gruyère de Comté, it is the French version of Swiss Gruyère, a delicious, nutty semifirm cheese made from unpasteurized cow's milk.

Mushrooms grow in abundance in the Franche-Comté region, which borders Switzerland.

It was one of the first French cheeses to receive AOC (page 31) recognition. Comté is a popular cheese for cooking as it melts nicely, and in this area of France it appears in fondue, cheese tarts, *gougères* and other pastries, and numerous chicken and meat dishes.

Regional Specialties

Dandelion greens Picked from the dandelion plant, these slightly bitter greens are usually enjoyed as a salad

Les gaudes Cousin to polenta, this cornmeal porridge is eaten hot or is cooled and sliced

Brési Thinly sliced beef that has been salted, dried, and smoked in a fireplace; similar to Italian *bresaola*

Saucisse de Morteau AOC (page 31) smoked pork sausages, typically accompanied by crusty fried *rösti* potatoes

Raclette Typical mountain dish of salted cow's milk cheese placed near an open fire and scraped onto potatoes as it melts

Brochette Pieces of cheese wrapped in ham, skewered, and fried

Poulet au Vin Jaune Chicken and morel mushrooms in a creamy sauce made with local white wine

Sauce Nantua Béchamel-like white sauce that includes crayfish or shrimp (prawns), usually served with egg or seafood dishes

Vin de Paille "Straw wine," a velvety, dark amber dessert wine made from grapes spread on straw and aged for a few months before the juices are extracted

Vin Jaune "Yellow wine," a sweet dessert wine made from Sauvignon grapes in a process similar to that used for producing sherry and cask-aged for six to ten years

LANGUEDOC-ROUSSILLON

Land of the Midday Sun

Languedoc-Roussillon, a coastal region in southeastern France, was historically a province of far greater importance than it is today. It was a political center of the Midi, or southern France, and its great port at Agde was founded by the Greeks. Invaders were common on the Mediterranean coast, so Languedoc hill towns are often walled, and its churches resemble fortresses. The ancient capital of Languedoc, Toulouse, now part of the Midi-Pyrénées region, is a great eating city, and its modern-day capital, Montpellier, was an important hub in the spice trade.

The food of Languedoc-Roussillon has a solid, down-to-earth character and is Mediterranean at heart. The menu term *à la languedocienne* indicates a combination of tomatoes, eggplant (aubergine), and porcini (cèpes) mushrooms, seasoned with garlic. Languedoc is a region of great geographical contrasts. Although it is a coastal region, the interior is mountainous and travel is difficult, which explains the surprising popularity of salt cod. In the Cévennes Mountains, aromatic herbs grow wild on high arid plateaus and give flavor to the lamb that grazes there and to the local honey. Descending to the fertile low country around Montpellier, the scene shifts to pastoral wine country. Languedoc has been an important grape-growing region for centuries, although until recently its wines earned little respect. Thanks to entrepreneurial efforts in the 1970s and 1980s, the region now makes some well-regarded AOC (page 31) wines, particularly Corbières and Côtes du Roussillon Villages.

East along the coast lies the cattle country of the Camargue, the marshy delta of the Rhône River where Languedoc meets Provence. Roussillon, to the west, includes many mountain settlements in the eastern Pyrenees, where Catalan is spoken and the food displays a decidedly Spanish flair with the use of sweet peppers, saffron, and citrus.

Culinary Signature: Cassoulet

Cassoulet, whose name stems from an earthenware pot called a *cassolo*, is a classic dish of Languedoc that long ago became common all over southwestern France. The garlicky stew always includes white beans, tomatoes, goose fat, and an onion studded with cloves, but the meaty elements vary. The basic Castelnaudary version combines ham, pork shoulder, pork cracklings, and sausage. The version from the fortified city of Carcassonne adds a leg of mutton and perhaps partridge. The extravagant Toulouse-style cassoulet specifies all of the above plus bacon, white Toulouse sausage, and often confit leg of goose or duck. After long, slow simmering to meld the flavors and tenderize the meat, the stew is sprinkled with bread crumbs and baked until a crust forms.

Regional Specialties

Anchovies Harvested at Collioure and often added with garlic to mayonnaise

Sardines Enjoyed on the Mediterranean coast, often fried or grilled and served with a sauce

Red rice Brick red with a nutty flavor and firm texture, grown in the marshy Camargue

Beef The beef of the Camargue, specifically the deep red, gamy meat of the bull, is a newer addition to AOC (page 31) rosters

Fleur de sel Sea salt is gathered by hand near the Camargue; the town of Aigues-Mortes is particularly known for its salt beds

Brandade de morue Salt cod crushed into a paste with garlic, milk, and olive oil, sometimes garnished with truffles

Morue à la languedocienne Salt cod creamed together with potatoes and garlic

Bourride Monkfish stew with wine and vegetables, garnished with aioli; similar to bouillabaisse without the tomatoes and saffron

Poulard à la languedocienne Chicken stuffed with eggplant (aubergine), tomatoes, and porcini (cèpes) mushrooms

Boles de picoulat Meatballs made with onions and olives, served in an herbed tomato sauce

Saucisse à la catalane Roussillon dish made up of sausages fried with fresh herbs, garlic, and orange peel

Honey Many varieties are made, with flavors ranging from delicate heather to more heady herbs from the mountain plateaus

Cassoulet, a slow-cooked stew, is popular throughout southwestern France.

LIMOUSIN

Deep French Countryside

Like the Auvergne, Limousin is part of the Massif Central, the elevated region of mountains and plateaus of south-central France. Limousin primarily an agricultural region, provides wholesome foodstuffs for other parts of France: grain, fruit, nuts, eggs, mushrooms, sheep, and especially cattle (the Limousin breed has a distinctive red color). This is the sort of region that the French refer to as *la France profonde*, "deepest France," far from the influence of Paris and other cities. Limousin shares some typical ingredients with the Périgord, which it borders on the west, such as truffles and foie gras. However, most of the native dishes are less elegant than this implies. The indigenous cuisine is rough peasant food: the description *à la limousine* indicates that a dish includes steamed red cabbage or Brussels sprouts and braised chestnuts. Cornerstones of the traditional Limousin menu include soups made from oats, cabbage, and rye bread. As a reward for nearing the bottom of the bowl, diners traditionally poured a little red wine into the last few spoonfuls of soup, swirled the bowl, and drank the mixture—a gesture called *font chabro*t or *chabrol*.

Culinary Signature: Clafouti

This cakelike custard, enjoyed in many areas of France, originated in Limousin. Sometimes baked in a cast-iron frying pan, a clafouti may be dotted with stone fruits such as apricots or plums or berries such as blackberries or raspberries, but most traditionally with black cherries, which are left unpitted to add flavor. Like peach pits, cherry pits carry a slight bitter-almond flavor which add another dimension of flavor to the dessert.

Regional Specialties

Chestnuts Vast groves of chestnut trees make these meaty nuts a common addition to Limousin dishes, from blood sausage to chestnut crêpes

Mushrooms The forests of Limousin offer an array of mushrooms for foraging, including porcinis (cèpes), morels, and truffles

Bréjaude Garlic-flavored cabbage soup made with bacon and red wine

Lièvre en chabessal Hare stuffed with pork, veal, and ham, tied, and cooked in a round dish; a relative of *lièvre à la royale*, which adds foie gras and truffles to the mix and is claimed by several regions as their own

Millassous de pommes de terre Potato pie that also includes garlic, bacon, and herbs

Farcidures Potato and pork dumplings

Tourtous Buckwheat pancakes that once served as bread in the Limousin but are now mostly relegated to dessert

Flaugnarde Light clafouti, or custard cake, made in wintertime with apples or pears; also known as *flognard*

Violet mustard Purple-hued mustard that is made with mustard seeds and black grape must

Berries Raspberries, blueberries, strawberries, gooseberries, and black currants grow especially well in the Limousin and are used to make jams, tarts, pastries, and liqueurs

Madeleines The town of Saint-Yrieix is known for its rendition of these small cakes baked in a special pan with shell indentations

Clafouti is a custardlike dessert traditionally made with cherries, but other fruits may also be used.

LORRAINE

Robust Comfort Food

The northeasterly region of Lorraine shares borders with Belgium, Luxembourg, and Germany, and for many centuries was an independent duchy fought over and traded back and forth by France and Germany. A trace of these old divisions remains in the persistence of two capitals in Lorraine: Nancy and Metz. Although Germanic influence can be seen in Lorraine's cuisine, this region is essentially French—more so than its neighbor Alsace. Lorraine's cuisine has often turned to the west to borrow from the classic French cooking of Île-de-France. Lorraine's food is homey and hearty, represented in the French imagination by potato and red cabbage *à la lorraine,* or cooked in red wine. The potatoes of Breux are known for their high quality, and smoked bacon is a specialty of the region, making an appearance in most of the classic Lorraine dishes. Lorraine also claims to have invented both the madeleine and the macaroon. Vineyards on the Moselle River near Metz produce white wine as well as *vin gris,* gray wine, white wine made from Gamay or Pinot Noir grapes. Along with Alsace, Lorraine produces some of the best beer in France.

Culinary Signature: Quiche Lorraine

This savory pie of egg, cream, and *lardons* (small strips of pork fat) encased in a flaky crust is traditionally baked in a cast-iron pan. The simplest version is the most classic, but sometimes Gruyère or Emmentaler cheese and onions are added, although technically this transforms the dish into a *quiche alsacienne.*

Regional Specialties

Potée lorraine Hearty stew of pork breast and leg, carrots, turnips, leek, cabbage, and bacon
Pâté lorrain Mixture of chopped pork and

Quiche Lorraine, named after the region where it originated, is made up of eggs, cream, and bacon.

veal moistened with white wine and encased in puff pastry
Tourte à la lorraine Egg-and-cream tart with veal and pork
Boudin noir The blood sausages of Nancy are widely admired, as is the andouille, or tripe sausage, of the Val d'Ajol
Jams and jellies Gooseberry and currant are local favorites
Ramequin This sweet flour and milk cake was originally a cheesecake but evolved into something lighter
Macaroons Of Italian origin, these meringue-like almond cookies are a specialty of Nancy
Madeleines Buttery almond cookielike cakes scented with orange water, a specialty of the town of Commercy

Eaux-de-vie Lorraine is great country for fruit brandies, including *mirabelle,* from small yellow plums; *quetsch* from large purple plums; kirsch from cherries; and, most popular of all, framboise from raspberries

MIDI-PYRÉNÉES

A Modern Patchwork

One of France's artificial regions without true historical or geographical unity, Midi-Pyrénées was created in the 1970s. Situated between Aquitaine and Languedoc, it includes parts of historic Gascony and Languedoc, even subsuming the ancient Languedocian capital of Toulouse. Not surprisingly, the cuisine shares elements with the cuisines of those two regions, as well

the south. Although the Midi-Pyrénées produces quality wines, they are often overshadowed by Bordeaux to the west.

Culinary Signature: Roquefort

The famous limestone caves of Roquefort, historically possessed by Languedoc, now belong to the Midi-Pyrénées. The damp, drafty environment of the caves favors the development of the mold *Penicillium roquefortii* which gives this blue cheese a flavor like no other, an excellent illustration of the impact of *terroir* on cheese. The sheep's milk used to make Roquefort is gathered from a wide area reaching into other regions, but the milk must be brought to the Roquefort caves for aging. In 1925, Roquefort was distinguished as the first cheese awarded AOC (page 31) status.

Regional Specialties

Aligout Dish of mashed potatoes and cheese similar to the *aligot* of the Auvergne, but also including tomatoes

Alicot Stew of goose or duck simmered with porcini (cèpes) mushrooms and roasted chestnuts, not to be confused with *aligout*

Garbure Thick stew made of cabbage, potatoes, beans, pork, stale bread, and sometimes goose leg confit

Boudin blanc In the Quercy area this white colored pork sausage is made with pork cheeks and truffles

Omelette aux cèpes Growing wild in this area and easier to find than truffles, porcinis (cèpes) are a popular addition to omelettes

Tripoux This dish of sheep tripe, stuffed with sheep feet and sweetbreads and braised with vegetables, sometimes shows a Catalan influence in the use of saffron

Gâteau à la broche Spongy batter cake spit-roasted before an open fire, a specialty of the Pyrénées

Anise-flavored fennel is prepared with raisins and saffron, an influence from Spain.

as with the mountain cuisines of the Massif Central and the Pyrénées. Drawing on the rich natural resources of southwest France, the food here is hearty and flavorful. The goose used throughout France for foie gras originally comes from Toulouse, and both confit and black truffles play as important a role here as they do to the west in the Périgord. Since a section of historic Languedoc is now part

of this region, Midi-Pyrénées can also claim cassoulet as its own. The northeastern part of Midi-Pyrénées covers the ancient province of Rouergue, part of the Massif Central, where the game birds are famously delicious thanks to the wild mountain juniper and thyme they feed on. The cuisine also shares many aspects with that of the Auvergne. The Catalan dishes enjoyed in Roussillon are also found in the Pyrénées to

NORD–PAS DE CALAIS

The French Netherlands

This northerly region on the Belgian border that includes Flanders and part of the forest of Ardennes has historically been an area of strategic military importance, much fought over and traded back and forth by various European powers. Once dominated by the Netherlands, it definitively became part of France relatively late and retains strong cultural ties with the Low Countries. The Flemish influence is clear in the cuisine. Mackerel and herring are popular and found in many preserved forms, but aside from a couple of signature seafood dishes (and despite the coastline), the menu is heavy on meat. The vegetables here tend toward humble and hearty: the French menu term *à la flamande* indicates a garnish of braised cabbage, carrots, turnips, and potatoes, and sometimes pork or sausage. Lille is the region's capital, and here the beer flows as wine does in other French cities. The cheeses from this far northern part of France, such as Belgian Limburger, are fruity, strong flavored, and are quite pungent.

Culinary Signature: Endive

Nord–Pas de Calais is one of the world's best areas for growing Belgian endive, also known as French endive or witloof. As is done with asparagus in this part of the world, the plants are kept pale by depriving them of light as they grow, a process known as *etoliation*. Only the tips of the leaves are left exposed, so they are typically green or purple-red rather than white. Belgian endive is crisp and bitter, and may be stuffed, eaten raw in a salad, or cooked in a gratin. Other members of the chicory family, also popular in this area, are curly endive, also called frisée, and broad-leafed endive, or escarole.

Regional Specialties

Smoked garlic In Arleux, garlic woven into long braids by raffia is hung and smoked for ten days over a peat fire

Andouillette de Cambrai Tripe sausage, served roasted or grilled with apples

Carbonnade à la flamande Sweet-sour stew of beef cooked in beer with onions, vinegar, brown sugar or red currant jelly, and spices

Hochepot Peasant stew of pig ear and tail, mutton, beef, and oxtail with root vegetables and cabbage

Coq à la bière In this region, beer, *bière*, is substituted for the wine in coq au vin

Caudière Cream-based seafood stew that contains mussels and onions

Waterzoï Type of bouillabaisse, made with cold-water fish from the English Channel, whose broth is finished with cream, butter, carrots, leeks, potatoes and herbs

Escavêche Terrine made of cold-water fish, wine, and vinegar

Tarte de Maroilles A quichelike custard tart classically made with pungent Maroilles cheese, leeks, and sometimes including an upper crust

Gaufres fourées Crisp Belgian-style waffles that are sometimes filled with vanilla cream

Bêtises de Cambrai These popular hard mint candies flavored with a ribbon of caramelized sugar were supposedly created as a *bêtise*, "mistake," by an apprentice confectioner in the town of Cambrai

Beer Served in Flemish bars called *estaminets* that are located throughout the region; signature styles are *blanche*, or wheat beer; *gueuze*, a Belgian-style lambic beer; and Trois Monts, a type of ale

Genièvre Juniper-flavored liquor borrowed from nearby Belgium

In Nord–Pas de Calais, colorful endive is an adopted favorite from nearby Belgium.

NORMANDY (NORMANDIE)

Land of Cream and Apples

Normandy is a characterful region of fertile farmland and bracing sea breezes. Nature has blessed Normandy with distinctive and delicious natural ingredients, and its capital, Rouen, is one of France's great eating cities. The chilly climate makes the region's apples, and the beverages produced from them, deservedly famous, and the rich, fatty milk of brown-and-white Normandy cows makes superior cream and butter that appear in many of the region's dishes. Many of the best-known French soft cheeses originated here, including Camembert. The proximity to the English Channel, which the French call *La Manche*, "the sleeve," means a menu rich in fish and shellfish, especially Dover sole, oysters, and mussels. Here, lambs and sheep graze on salty fields, *prés sales*, which gives their meat a sought-after distinctive parsley flavor.

Apples reign supreme in Normandy. Their versatility lends them to salads, desserts, and even brandy.

Culinary Signature: Apples

Apples grow well in many elevated regions of France and in the colder regions north of the Loire River, but nowhere better than in Normandy. Here, the apple replaces the grape, and the Normans drink hard cider as if it were wine. They also distill cider into Calvados, an apple brandy, and were once famous for their habit of drinking a shot partway through a meal to create room for more food—making, as they indelicately put it, *le trou normand*, "the Norman hole". Apples also appear in both savory and sweet dishes, from omelettes to the *tarte normande*, or apple tart, and pair especially well with the wonderfully rich, creamy cheeses of Normandy.

Regional Specialties

Butter Excellent butter comes from Isigny, Cormeilles, and Neufchâtel in particular, some bearing the AOC (see page 31) label

Andouilles de Vire Smoked, cooked pork-and-tripe sausages, traditionally served in thin slices with country bread and cider

Moules à la crème Mussels cooked with cream and cider

Canard à la rouennaise Duck stuffed with its liver and cooked in red wine

Omelettes Popular dishes, even including sweet ones; a classic favorite includes apples, Calvados, and cream

Sole à la normande Sole simmered in cream

Tripes à la mode de Caen Tripe cooked with cider and Calvados

Brioche Some claim that this light and airy bread originated in the town of Gournay

Fleur de sel As in Brittany, salt is gathered off the Normandy coast, notably at Isigny

Caramels d'Isigny Salted butter toffee from Isigny, made with AOC Isigny cream

Tarte normande Apples baked in a rich vanilla custard and puff-pastry shell

Calvados, an apple brandy, is enjoyed as an *apéritif* and is used in desserts such as sorbet.

Cider Hard apple cider replaces wine in Normandy, both as an accompaniment to food and for cooking

Calvados Eau-de-vie distilled from apple cider

Pommeau *Apéritif* made from Calvados mixed with apple must or unfermented cider

Bénédictine An aromatic herbal liqueur produced at Fécamp Abbey since 1510

PARIS–ISLE OF FRANCE (ÎLE-DE-FRANCE)

The Heart of France

Along with Centre, Paris–Isle of France is the green heartland of France: the lush, fertile countryside is graced with gently rolling green hills, vineyards, farms, forests, and streams, and at its center lies the city of Paris. The region is called the Isle of France because five rivers carve it out into a near island in the middle of the country: the Epte to the northwest, the Eure and Yonne to the southwest, the Marne to the east, and the Aisne to the northeast. This region is part of the "garden of France," known for its mushrooms or *champignons de Paris*, apples from Faro, pears from Groslay, and asparagus from Argenteuil, as well as peas, cauliflower, artichokes, white Chevrier beans, strawberries, and cherries, especially those from Montmorency. The area is so closely identified with fresh garden produce that the term *à la parisienne* means accompanied with tiny vegetables sautéed in butter and sprinkled with parsley. However, at the other extreme, the Parisian region was also the birthplace of haute cuisine and modern restaurant culture. For centuries, gastronomy was developed and honed here in royal and noble kitchens, drawing talented cooks from all over France to the area. Unlike in other regions of France, the great dishes of the Île-de-France are not regional specialties based on particular native ingredients, but often singular inventions by an individual chef.

Culinary Signature: Baguette

Paris enjoys a bounty of great *boulangeries*, or bread shops, but no other bread is as closely identified with the city as the baguette. This long, slender loaf made of lean dough is known for its crisp golden crust and chewy crumb. Baguettes are baked in specialized trays in a hot, steamy oven and sport diagonal slashes on the top of the loaves, which help the bread expand.

Regional Specialties

Jambon de Paris Mild, lightly salted, unsmoked ham enjoyed on a baguette with butter; known as *sandwich jambon*

Meaux mustard Rustic cousin of Dijon mustard, made with vinegar, crushed or whole mustard seeds, and spices

Paris–Isle of France is the heartland of France where vegetables are grown in abundance.

French onion soup Classic soup based on onions and beef broth, topped with a crouton and cheese and then put under the broiler to achieve a golden crust

Potage Saint-Germain Puréed pea soup named after the Saint-Germain arrondissement (or district) in Paris

Potage Crécy Carrot soup, traditionally from carrots harvested in the nearby village of Crécy

Potage aux primeurs Spring vegetable soup created by foreign minister Talleyrand's famed chef, Marie Antoine Carême

Matelote Freshwater fish or eel cooked in wine with mushrooms and onions

Steak frites Steak and fries, a Parisian bistro classic; several choices of steak are usually offered, the preferred one being *entrecôte*, or rib steak, and the meat is properly served *saignant*, "rare"

Oysters can be found in every town along the extensive French coastline.

Huîtres Marenne-Oléron Oysters from Marenne-Oléron, a famous oyster-farming region on the Atlantic coast, are small and delicate with a clean flavor

Beurre Poitou-Charentes Butter produced from raw cream in Échiré has been awarded AOC status (page 31) for its outstanding flavor

Matelote d'anguilles Eel stew

Broyé poitevin A simple butter and egg cake that is rolled flat before baking and broken rather than sliced

Macarons de Montmorillon This town in the Vienne department is famous for its little crown-shaped macaroons

Cognac No ordinary brandy, Cognac is made with Charente grapes in the area of the same name

Pineau des Charentes Sweet fortified wine, the result of adding Cognac to unfermented wine must; enjoyed as an *apéritif*

here (as elsewhere along the Atlantic and north coasts of France) on wooden stakes or ropes, called bouchots, which are submerged at high tide but exposed to the sea air at low tide. This process slows the mussels' growth, improves flavor, and leaves no gritty sediment in their shells. Locals claim that their mussels are sweeter than those of Brittany or Normandy because of the slightly warmer water. Some of the most characteristic dishes of this region revolve around mussels. Every menu offers steamed mussels with white wine, seawater, and a dollop of crème fraîche. Then there is *mouclade,* a creamy mussel stew, generally spiked with curry or saffron. The *éclade des moules,* a clambake with mussels, often takes place on beaches on the Île de Ré just off the coast from La Rochelle. Pine planks are soaked in seawater and the mussels are arranged on them in a circular pattern with the hinged sides up and covered with pine needles. The pine needles are set aflame and burn for just a few minutes, bathing the mussels in woodsy smoke to just cook them before they are enjoyed directly from the shell with country bread, butter, and white wine.

Regional Specialties

Fleur de sel Some of France's best sea salt is gathered off the Atlantic coast around the Île de Ré and Île d'Oléron

Mojhette Local white beans grown in marshes, often the product of small-scale market gardens

Potatoes The ones from the Île de Ré have been granted AOC status (page 31) for their unique flavor of salt air

PROVENCE

The Enchanting South

Just as Alsace shares much in common with Germany, and Brittany with Wales, Provence is the most Italian region of France. This sunny southeastern land, which extends from the Alps to the Mediterranean and includes the great vineyards bordering the Rhône River, is known for the warmth of its people, the vibrant flavors of its food, and the unrivaled beauty of its landscape, dotted with olive trees. The charms of this region are many and varied: the bustling seaport of Marseilles; the charming, laid-back, sun-drenched city of Nice; the glamorous Riviera; the colorful fields of mustard and lavender around Arles; the rugged foothills of Haute-Provence. The cuisine is varied, too ranging from the cheeses and rustic mountain

RHÔNE-ALPES

Charcuterie Plate

•

Celery Root Rémoulade

Beef Brisket with Sauce Gribiche

Frisee Salad with Poached Egg
and Lardons

Côtes du Rhône

BURGUNDY

Gruyère Gougères

•

Coq au Vin

Butter Lettuce with Dijon Vinaigrette

White Burgundy

PROVENCE

Pissaladière

•

Provençal Beef Stew

Ratatouille

Châteauneuf-du-Pape

•

Tarte au Citron

BRITTANY

Miniature Savory Buckwheat Crêpes

•

Lamb with Flageolet Beans

Cidrae

•

Almond Pound Cake

AQUITAINE

Pork Pâté

•

Seared Tuna with Pipérade

Sauvignon Blanc

•

Chocolate Soufflés

Eating the French Way

Even French families that have lived in the city for generations possess a deep, ingrained love of the land and respect for the seasons. Many maintain a habit of visiting the country on weekends and gathering for a big Sunday lunch with various generations of their relatives.

The pace of daily life has increased in France as elsewhere, but the French remain very passionate about food and are continuing to find ways to meld their beloved culinary traditions with the new modern way of life.

CHOOSE FRESH INGREDIENTS

The French are famously picky about ingredients. Even today, when fewer people have time to spend hours in the kitchen preparing the midday and evening meals, many still keep up the old custom of shopping once daily, if not twice. They eschew the *supermarché* (or, worse, the *hypermarché*) in favor of visiting specialty purveyors of meat, poultry, seafood, cheese, bread, and vegetables. Or they stop at a local farmers' market. Vendors expect to be questioned thoroughly about the origins and quality of their wares, and the final choice of which dish to cook for dinner will often be determined after a dialogue with the grocer and the customer about what items are best and freshest that day.

This sort of flexibility and openness makes for delicious meals during a busy work week, yet for entertaining or for a weekend family lunch, more advance planning is in order. The right ingredients must be located for the recipes on the menu, but when time is allowed for leisurely and organized preparation, creating an elaborate meal can be a pleasurable experience for the cook.

PREPARE IN ADVANCE

The French were the first to codify the art and science of professional cooking, and one of the basic tenets of every modern professional kitchen is a French term: *la mise en place.* Literally "the putting in place," it refers to the measuring and preparation of ingredients in an orderly fashion before the cooking begins. A French chef relies on a battery of sous-chefs to chop onions, prepare confit of duck leg, and simmer veal demi-glace before he or she approaches the stove to create a culinary masterpiece. This elementary concept is not applied just to the preparation of haute cuisine. Every home cook, whether a novice or expert in the kitchen, can benefit from the same commonsense practice. Even the most creative, instinctual cook can enjoy the process of cooking even more when the task begins with a clean kitchen; ingredients washed, chopped, and otherwise made ready; and all the utensils the cook needs accounted for and placed within easy reach.

Although the term usually applies to ingredients for a particular dish, *mise en place* also pertains to the dishes that are combined to create a meal. For a typical big French meal, the cook will try to prepare as much of the food as possible in advance, avoiding a last-minute flurry. If the main dish will require quick sautéing or creating a pan sauce just before serving, the other dishes on the menu will be ones that can be finished ahead of time and set aside just until serving. Some of the dishes closest to the French heart—pâtés, pots-au-feu and braises—are ones that can be prepared and cooked well in advance of serving, and in fact improve in flavor when allowed to sit for a day or two. This makes them ideal for entertaining, giving you more time and attention to devote to your guests.

The lavish farmers' markets of Paris are famous for their outstanding seasonal fruits and vegetables.

the cook tosses and turns it, and the angled handle helps the cook jerk and shake the pan with ease. Sauté pans, unlike frying pans, are fitted with lids, which are useful for steaming foods after they are browned and simmering (which is done without the lid). A sauté pan can also be used to braise foods on the stovetop.

Saucepan

The sides of this basic round pan are high and either quite straight or slightly sloped, depending on the intended use. Flared and sometimes rounded pans, also called *sauciers*, increase the exposed surface of a liquid and encourage rapid evaporation to concentrate a sauce. Straight sides allow a sauce to simmer without evaporating too quickly. Basic, straight-sided saucepans come with lids.

Crêpe Pan

To make crêpes the French way, you need a flat crêpe pan, which has a long handle set at a high angle to help you roll and tilt the pan as you swirl butter and then batter over the bottom to make a very thin pancake. Low, flared sides make it easy to flip the crêpe to cook the second side. Crêpe pans are sold in several sizes and can have a nonstick or steel surface. One that is 10 inches (25 cm) in diameter is the most common.

Stockpot

Big enough to accommodate a large volume of simmering stock and tall and narrow enough to let it cook for hours without evaporating away too much, a stockpot is the perfect vessel for making homemade stocks as well as large batches of soups It is also practical for cooking pasta. The best stockpots are made with heavy metal, which promotes heat conduction and efficient cooking, and also have sturdy handless. Most also come with lids.

Specialty pans such as this one for Pommes Anna are made specifically for the dishes they are named after.

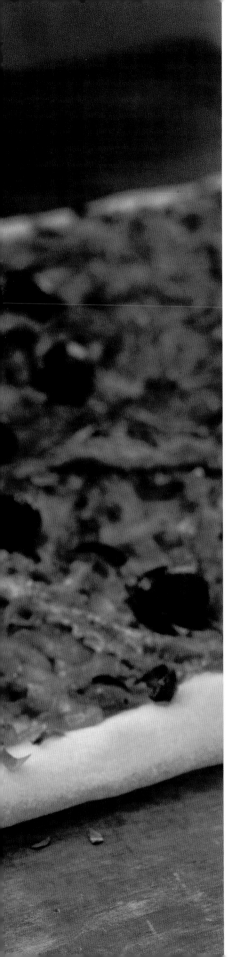

Hors d'Oeuvres

About Hors d'Oeuvres

One of the most delightful and civilized customs of the French table, the hors d'oeuvre, literally "outside the work," goes hand in hand with the *apéritif* and smoothly ushers in a meal, awakening the appetite and preparing the palate for more pleasures to come.

Often enjoyed twice a day, before lunch and before dinner, the hors d'oeuvre and *apéritif* are more than just a first course. In fact, they may not even occur at the table. The French will stop at a café on the way home for a glass of wine and a nibble. Or, neighbors will invite one another to their homes for a bite and a pastis, just a brief but pleasurable visit that does not include the actual meal. This interlude helps diners transition from the busy workday to an evening of relaxation with family and friends, and engaging conversation around the dining table.

Hors d'oeuvres are usually intensely flavored tidbits that leave you hungry for more. Simple, easy-to-prepare appetizers include marinated olives, raw vegetables with a dip, cheese and crackers, and sliced purchased meats such as sausage and boiled ham. For more elaborate appetizers, cooks make homemade pâtés and terrines. In coastal areas, seafood preparations such as raw oysters on the half-shell (page 71) or *brandade*, a luscious salt cod spread (page 73), are favored. High-end restaurants sometimes offer an *amuse-bouche*—a dainty, stylized hors d'oeuvre that may be devoured in one bite, simply to "amuse the mouth" and tantalize the taste buds for the meal to come.

STRATEGIC MEAL PLANNING

When deciding on an hors d'oeuvre to start a meal, first consider the season and availability of ingredients. Vegetables should be at their natural peak of ripeness, so you'll want to enjoy classic hors d'oeuvres such as Celery Root Rémoulade (page 60) in the wintertime. Radishes with Butter and Sea Salt (page 72) is a quintessential springtime pleasure, while Goat Cheese, Leek, and Mushroom Tart (page 55) is best in autumn, when many fresh mushrooms are at their peak and readily available in markets.

Another consideration is the regionality of the entire meal. A simple hors d'oeuvre like Herring Marinated in Olive Oil and Fresh Herbs (page 70) is associated with northern France, making it a perfect introduction to other dishes typical of that part of the country, such as Chard Gratin (page 187) or Endive Salad (page 98). A number of hors d'oeuvres highlight the flavors of southern France: *palmiers,* the elegant pastries filled with the olive spread known as tapenade (page 63), and crudités, a selection of cooked and raw vegetables served with the renowned garlic mayonnaise, aioli (page 59). Gruyère Gougères (page 56), small, light cheese puffs, are a classic in Burgundy and make a fitting prelude to Beef Bourguignon (page 149). Crêpes are a hallmark of Breton cuisine, so start off a meal featuring another traditional Breton dish, such as Lamb with Flageolet Beans (page 168), with Miniature Savory Buckwheat Crêpes (page 64) topped with crème fraîche and fresh chives.

Yet another factor to consider in your planning is the time you want to spend in the kitchen. A multi-course meal with several complex dishes calls for the simplest hors d'oeuvre. If you live near a good cheese shop or specialty grocer, follow the French custom and purchase a selection of cheeses and charcuterie (page 48), and serve them with toasts, or *croûtes,* as well as olives and a variety of nuts. In warm months especially, keep in mind that serving a room-temperature hors d'oeuvre minimizes last-minute preparations in the kitchen. However, if the main dish is a braise, a stew, or a similar make-ahead meal, you have more time to assemble an hors d'oeuvre like *pissaladière,* the iconic onion tart of Provence (page 52).

Some signature French hors d'oeuvres must be prepared in advance. Foie Gras Terrine (page 66), Pork Rillettes (page 67), and Pork Pâté (page 69) are prepared and then refrigerated for days or even weeks to allow their distinctive flavors and textures to develop. When ready to serve, each of these recipes needs only to be paired with toasts or bread and it will be ready to enjoy.

THE APÉRITIF

The French hors d'oeuvre would be lacking without a beverage to accompany it. The best *apéritifs* enhance the appetite and excite the palate for the meal that lies ahead.

The accompanying beverage can simply be a glass of white wine, Champagne, or red wine. Add a splash of crème de cassis or black currant liqueur to make, respectively, a Kir, a Kir Royale, and a Communard. Liqueurs flavored with blackberry, or *mûre,* and peach, or *pêche,* may also be used. Anise-flavored *apéritifs,* such as pastis, are popular in southern France, as they are elsewhere in the Mediterranean region. The hors d'oeuvres here would also be complemented by a slightly sweet fortified wine such as sherry, a good vermouth, or Pineau des Charentes; the herbaceous red Dubonnet; and the citrusy white Lillet, or the sweeter Lillet Rouge.

La Charcuterie

In both homes and restaurants in every region of France, one of the most common starters to a meal is a platter of assorted charcuterie, or cured meats. The charcuterie plate is accompanied by olives, cornichons, and bread and butter along with an *apéritif* or glass of wine.

GATHERING THE INGREDIENTS
First, decide on the number of guests you'll be serving and what dishes will follow after the charcuterie plate. If you are serving a multi-course meal, you may want to go with a lighter selection of meats; if you are serving small plates or appetizers only, you will want a heartier selection. Choose a variety of meats that have different textures (see descriptions

on next page). For example, rillettes are a creamy spread, thinly sliced *saucisson* adds a chewy component, and a pâté or terrine can range in texture from a silky smooth mixture to a blended chunky one.

After you have decided on the meats, choose the accompaniments. Always offer a few nonmeat options to round out the plate, such as brined or oil-cured olives, nuts, slices

of bread, or cornichons. Butter is rarely offered with bread in France, but always appears when charcuterie is served.

PREPARING THE PLATE
After you have made your charcuterie plate selections, begin arranging them on a large decorative platter or wooden serving board. Spreads such as pâtés and rillettes should be placed in small crocks, as should olives and butter. Sausages and other meats and breads should be thinly sliced.

Prepare the platter just before you are ready to serve so that the meat doesn't sit out too long and the bread remains fresh.

CHARCUTERIE COMPONENTS

Terrine Pâté (see below) named after the container in which it is made. The containers are usually rectangular or oval and made of heavy earthenware or enameled iron.

Jambon Blanc Ham that has been brined and then boiled and sliced very thin. Also common are *jambon cru* (salt-cured ham) and *jambon fumé* (smoked ham). All should be served slightly cold or at room temperature.

Saucisson Sausage that is usually air-dried and sliced very thin. Other classic types of sausage are andouille (tripe sausage) or the smaller version called *andouillette*, *boudin blanc* (white sausage made from chicken, veal, or pork), and *boudin noir* (dark sausage made from pork blood). All should be served at room temperature.

Rillettes Rich spread of shredded meat such as pork, duck, or goose, or more rarely, chicken or turkey. Sometimes covered with aspic.

Pâté Chopped and ground (minced) meat mixture that can range in texture from silky smooth to chunky and rustic. It can be made from almost any meat or combination of meat, the most common being pork, veal, and rabbit.

Accompaniments Niçoise or Picholine olives, cornichons, butter, baguette, cheeses, and snails filled with garlic butter.

Crottin Tartines with Mango Chutney

Crottin de Chavignol (page 217) is the best known of the small, round goat cheeses called *crottins* that are typical in France. In restaurants and homes throughout the country, these cheeses are warmed and used as an ingredient in composed salads and to make quick hors d'oeuvres like this one. Here, mango chutney is used to top the *tartines*, or toasts, but a bit of Tapenade (page 270), Anchoïade (page 269), or honey also complements the goat cheese. Look for *crottins* that are soft on the inside with a slight crust on the outside.

Preheat the oven to 400°F (200°C).

Arrange the baguette slices in a single layer on a rimmed baking sheet and brush both sides with the olive oil. Bake until lightly golden on the first side, about 12 minutes. Turn the baguette slices over and bake until lightly golden on the second side, 6–7 minutes longer. Set aside.

Preheat the broiler (grill). Line a baking sheet with aluminum foil.

Using a sharp knife, cut each cheese round horizontally into slices ¼ inch (6 mm) thick. Place the slices, cut side down, on the prepared baking sheet. Broil (grill) the cheese just until the edges melt slightly, about 3 minutes.

Arrange the toasted baguette slices on a platter. Using a spatula, place a cheese round, cut side down, on top of each slice. Top each *tartine* with a dollop of chutney. Serve warm, passing the remaining chutney on the platter.

8 baguette slices, each about ¼ inch (6 mm) thick

1–2 tablespoons extra-virgin olive oil

2 rounds Crottin de Chavignol cheese

⅓ cup (4 oz/125 g) prepared mango chutney

MAKES 4 SERVINGS

Pissaladière

For the dough

**2 packages (about
5 teaspoons) active dry yeast**

1 teaspoon sugar

1 teaspoon salt

**2 tablespoons extra-virgin
olive oil**

**3–3¹/₂ cups (15–17¹/₂ oz/
470–545 g) all-purpose
(plain) flour, plus extra
for dusting**

For the onion confit

**4 tablespoons cold unsalted
butter, cut into pieces**

**3¹/₂ lb (1.75 kg) yellow
onions, thinly sliced**

**1 bay leaf, torn into
2 or 3 pieces**

4 large sprigs fresh thyme

4 sprigs fresh winter savory

**1 teaspoon freshly ground
pepper**

¹/₂ teaspoon salt

**4 tablespoons (2 fl oz/60 ml)
extra-virgin olive oil**

**20 anchovy fillets packed
in olive oil**

20 oil-cured black olives

**2 tablespoons extra-virgin
olive oil**

**2 tablespoons minced
fresh marjoram**

MAKES 20 SERVINGS

To make the dough, in a small bowl, dissolve the yeast in 1 cup (8 fl oz/250 ml) warm water (100°–110°F/38°–43°C). Add the sugar and let stand until foamy, about 5 minutes. In a food processor, combine the yeast mixture, salt, 1 tablespoon of the olive oil, and 3 cups (15 oz/470 g) of the flour. Process until the ingredients come together into a ball. If the dough is too wet, add the remaining ¹/₂ cup (2¹/₂ oz/75 g) flour, as needed, until a smooth, firm ball forms. If the dough is too dry, slowly drizzle in a few drops of warm water until the ball forms. Continue to process until the dough is silky but firm, 3–4 minutes. Turn out the dough onto a well-floured work surface and knead until smooth and elastic, 4–5 minutes.

Coat a large bowl with the remaining 1 tablespoon olive oil. Place the dough in the bowl and turn to coat with the oil. Cover with a damp kitchen towel and let rise in a warm place until the dough doubles in bulk, 1–1¹/₂ hours. Punch down the dough, re-cover the bowl with the towel, and let rest for 30 minutes.

Meanwhile, make the onion confit: Position a rack in the upper third of the oven and preheat to 350°F (180°C). Place the butter pieces in a shallow baking dish large enough to hold all of the onions in a layer 1–1¹/₂ inches (2.5–4 cm) deep. Place the dish in the preheated oven. When the butter has melted, after about 5 minutes, remove the dish from the oven. Place half of the onions in the dish and add 1–2 pieces of bay leaf over the onions. Add 2 each of the thyme and winter savory sprigs and sprinkle with ¹/₂ teaspoon of the pepper and ¹/₄ teaspoon of the salt. Drizzle with 2 tablespoons of the olive oil. Repeat with the remaining onions, herbs, seasonings, and olive oil. Bake, turning the onions about every 10 minutes, until they are lightly golden brown and have reduced by nearly half, 1¹/₂–2 hours. Remove and discard the bay leaf pieces, thyme, and winter savory.

Raise the oven temperature to 500°F (260°C). Dust a 12 by 18 inch (30 by 45 cm) rimmed baking sheet with flour.

Punch down the dough and turn it out onto a floured work surface. Roll out the dough into a rectangle about 19 by 13 inches (48 by 33 cm). Transfer the dough to the prepared baking sheet and press up the sides of the dough to make a rim. Spread the onion confit over the dough and top with the anchovies and olives.

Bake until the bottom of the crust is crisp and the edges are lightly browned, 12–15 minutes. Drizzle with the olive oil and sprinkle with the marjoram.

Cut the tart into 20 rectangles. Serve warm or at room temperature.

This classic Provençal onion tart can be found in every *boulangerie,* or bakery, in every village in the south. Thick bread is topped with a golden layer of onions and garnished with salty black olives and anchovies. The French enjoy it as a meal on its own or as an hors d'oeuvre with rosé wine or pastis, both popular *apéritifs* in Provence.

Goat Cheese, Leek, and Mushroom Tart

A stand-by in French homes, savory tarts are often cut into small portions and served with an *apéritif*. The tarts are made by cooking vegetables such as leeks or onions, asparagus, or mushrooms, and then combining them with cheese or crème fraîche to make a smooth filling. The filling can be spread onto flatbread dough or sheets of puff pastry.

In a frying pan over medium-high heat, melt 2 tablespoons of the butter until it foams. Add the leeks and sauté until translucent, 4–5 minutes. Add the thyme, bay leaf, chicken stock, ½ teaspoon of the salt, and ½ teaspoon of the pepper. Reduce the heat to low, cover, and simmer until the leeks are nearly tender, about 15 minutes. Uncover and cook, stirring occasionally and being careful not to let the leeks brown, until almost all the liquid has evaporated, about 15 minutes longer. Remove and discard the bay leaf. Transfer the leeks to a bowl. Stir in the Crème Fraîche and goat cheese until well mixed.

In another frying pan over medium-high heat, melt the remaining 1 tablespoon butter until it foams. Add the mushrooms, the remaining ½ teaspoon salt, and the remaining ¼ teaspoon pepper and sauté until the mushrooms are soft and have released their juices, 3–4 minutes.

Preheat the oven to 400°F (200°C). Line a large rimmed baking sheet with parchment (baking) paper.

On a floured work surface, roll out the puff pastry into a rectangle 10 by 12 inches (25 by 30 cm) wide and ⅛ inch (3 mm) thick. Transfer the dough to the prepared baking sheet. Spread the leek mixture to within 1 inch (2.5 cm) of the edge of the dough and fold the edges of the dough over the filling to make a free-form tart. Bake until the crust puffs and both the crust and the leeks are golden, about 15 minutes. Scatter the mushrooms over the leeks and bake for 5 minutes longer.

Let the tart stand for 5–10 minutes. Cut into bite-size pieces and serve warm.

3 tablespoons unsalted butter

3 lb (1.5 kg) leeks, white parts and 1 inch (2.5 cm) of the pale green parts, thinly sliced

2 teaspoons fresh thyme leaves

1 bay leaf

½ cup (4 fl oz/125 ml) Chicken Stock (page 272) or chicken broth

1 teaspoon salt

¾ teaspoon freshly ground pepper

⅓ cup (3 fl oz/80 ml) Crème Fraîche (page 275 or purchased)

3 oz (90 g) soft goat cheese, crumbled

½ lb (250 g) mixed mushrooms such as oyster, chanterelle, and cremini, brushed clean and coarsely chopped

All-purpose (plain) flour for dusting

1 sheet puff pastry, thawed if frozen

MAKES 8–10 SERVINGS

Gruyère Gougères

⅓ cup (3 oz/90 g) unsalted butter

1 teaspoon salt

½ teaspoon freshly ground white pepper

Pinch of cayenne pepper

1 cup (5 oz/155 g) all-purpose (plain) flour

5 large eggs

1½ cups (6 oz/185 g) shredded Gruyère cheese

MAKES 8–10 SERVINGS

These delicate cheese puffs look deceptively fancy but are quite simple to prepare. Two types of pepper and cheese are added to a similar pastry dough used for éclairs and profiteroles, making *gougères* that are savory rather than sweet. For an extra flourish, cut the cooled puffs in half and fill them with a slice of charcuterie or a teaspoon of crab or shrimp (prawn) salad.

Preheat the oven to 425°F (220°C). Line 2 baking sheets with parchment (baking) paper. In a saucepan over medium-high heat, combine the butter, salt, white pepper, cayenne, and 1 cup (8 fl oz/250 ml) water and bring to a boil. Cook, stirring, until the butter melts, 3–4 minutes. Add the flour and, using a wooden spoon, mix vigorously until a thick paste forms and pulls away from the sides of the pan, about 3 minutes. Remove from the heat. Break 1 egg into the pan and, using the wooden spoon or an electric mixer, beat it into the batter until combined. Repeat with 3 additional eggs. Whisk in 1 cup (4 oz/125 g) of the cheese.

Dip a teaspoon into a glass of cold water, then scoop up a generous teaspoonful of the batter and push it onto the prepared baking sheet with a fingertip. Repeat with the remaining batter, spacing the *gougères* about 2 inches (5 cm) apart and dipping the spoon into the water each time to prevent sticking. Lightly beat the remaining egg. Brush the tops of the *gougères* with the beaten egg and sprinkle with the remaining ½ cup cheese, dividing evenly.

Bake for 10 minutes. Reduce the oven temperature to 350°F (180°C) and bake until the *gougères* are golden brown and crisp, about 15 minutes longer. Remove the baking sheets from the oven, pierce each *gougère* with a wooden skewer, and then return to the oven. Turn off the oven and leave the *gougères* in the oven for 10 minutes longer. Serve warm or at room temperature.

Crudités with Aioli

Aioli is the classic garlic mayonnaise beloved by the Provençal. It is used liberally with boiled vegetables, hard-boiled eggs (page 275), and salt cod when served as part of a *grand aioli*, but in a less elaborate presentation it is used as a dipping sauce for raw vegetables. Anchoïade (page 269) also makes a nice dipping sauce for crudités.

Place the beets in a saucepan with cold water to cover by 2 inches (5 cm) and bring to a boil over medium-high heat. Reduce the heat to medium, cover, and cook until the beets are easily pierced with a fork, 50–60 minutes. Drain the beets and rinse under running cold water. When the beets are cool enough to handle, peel the skins off and set aside.

Meanwhile, put the potatoes in another saucepan with cold water to cover by 2 inches (5 cm) and bring to a boil over medium-high heat. Reduce the heat to medium, cover, and cook until the potatoes are easily pierced with a fork, 15–20 minutes. Drain the potatoes and set aside to cool.

Peel the carrots, then cut into 3-inch (7.5-cm) lengths. Cut the black radishes into paper thin slices. Trim some of the leaves from the red radishes, leaving a few intact. Cut the celery stalks into 3-inch (7.5-cm) lengths. Cut the cooled potatoes in half or leave whole.

Arrange the beets, potatoes, carrots, black and red radishes, and celery on a platter. Put the Aioli in a bowl and set it on the platter. Serve at once.

3 red, yellow, or striped beets

6–8 baby potatoes such as Yukon gold, fingerling, or red

3 carrots

2 black radishes

12 small red radishes

4 stalks celery with leaves

1 cup (8 fl oz/250 ml) Aioli (page 271)

MAKES 4 SERVINGS

Celery Root Rémoulade

1 celery root (celeriac), about 1½ lb (750 g)

1 teaspoon salt

1 teaspoon fresh lemon juice

For the vinaigrette

¼ cup (2 oz/60 g) Dijon mustard

3 tablespoons boiling water

⅓–½ cup (3–4 fl oz/ 80–125 ml) mild extra-virgin olive oil

2 tablespoons white wine vinegar or Champagne vinegar

3 tablespoons minced fresh chives

Assorted crackers for serving

MAKES 4 SERVINGS

Using a vegetable peeler or sharp knife, cut the top from the celery root and discard. Cut away the rough, knobby skin from the celery root and discard. Using the thin slicing blade on a mandoline, cut the celery root crosswise into very thin slices. Then, using the knife and working on a cutting board, cut the slices into thin matchsticks.

In a large bowl, combine the celery root, salt, and lemon juice and toss to coat. Let stand for 30 minutes. Rinse the celery root under running cold water, drain, and pat dry with paper towels. Set aside.

To make the vinaigrette, warm a large heatproof bowl with hot water, then dry it completely. Put the mustard in the bowl and slowly drizzle in the boiling water, whisking until incorporated. Whisking continuously, slowly drizzle in the olive oil to make a thick sauce. Slowly drizzle in the vinegar, whisking until incorporated.

Add the celery root and gently toss to coat. Cover and refrigerate for at least 3 hours or up to overnight.

Transfer the rémoulade to a serving bowl and garnish with the chives. Arrange the crackers on a serving plate. Serve at once.

Celery root has a rough, shaggy exterior, but beneath it lies crisp, ivory white flesh with an intense celery flavor. For this popular appetizer, julienned celery root is soaked briefly in a light brine and then combined with a creamy vinaigrette. Celery root rémoulade is frequently served as one of a trio of salads, the other two typically made from grated carrots and cooked beets respectively. Here, it shines on its own as a flavorful topping for crackers.

Tomato and Tapenade Palmiers

In markets and small *épiceries* throughout France, fresh or frozen puff pastry is readily available and home cooks avail themselves of it to prepare both sweets and savories. This quick and easy-to-make appetizer is prepared by spreading the pastry with tapenade, a favorite olive spread from Provence, then rolling it, slicing it, and baking the individual pastries. For a variation, you can substitute another savory filling such as Anchoïade (page 269) and add goat cheese and herbs.

Position a rack in the middle of the oven, and preheat the oven to 425°F (220°C). Line 2 rimmed baking sheets with parchment (baking) paper.

Mince the tomato halves. In a bowl, stir together the minced tomatoes, tapenade, and thyme. Season to taste with salt.

On a lightly floured work surface, roll out the pastry dough into a rectangle about 12 by 10 inches (30 by 25 cm) wide, and ¼ inch (6 mm) thick. Spread a thin layer of the tapenade mixture over the dough to ¼ inch of the edge. Roll the long ends toward each other until they meet in the center, making 2 snug rolls. To prevent the tops from spreading apart while baking, use a spoon to drizzle drops of water along the area where the dough meets and then press the two rolls together. Wrap in plastic wrap and refrigerate for 20 minutes.

Sprinkle a little water onto the prepared baking sheets. Cut the double roll crosswise into slices about ½ inch (12 mm) thick. Arrange the slices on the prepared baking sheets, spacing them about 1½ inches (4 cm) apart. Place the baking sheets in the freezer for 10 minutes.

Bake the pastries until puffed and golden, 15–20 minutes. Let the pastries cool slightly on the baking sheets and serve warm.

4 oil-packed sun-dried tomato halves

½ cup (4 oz/125 g) Tapenade (page 270)

½ teaspoon minced fresh thyme

Salt

1 sheet puff pastry, thawed if frozen

MAKES 6–8 SERVINGS

Miniature Savory Buckwheat Crêpes

2 large eggs

½–¾ cup (4–6 fl oz/ 125–180 ml) whole milk

½ cup (2½ oz/75 g) buckwheat flour

½ cup (2½ oz/75 g) all-purpose (plain) flour

¼ teaspoon salt

Crème Fraîche (page 275 or purchased) for serving

Snipped fresh chives for serving

MAKES 15–20 CRÊPES

In a blender or food processor, combine the eggs and ½ cup (4 fl oz/125 ml) of the milk and pulse until blended. Add the buckwheat and all-purpose flours and the salt and pulse to make a smooth batter. Pour the batter into a bowl, cover, and refrigerate for at least 2 hours or up to overnight.

When you are ready to cook the crêpes, stir the batter well; it will be thicker than traditional crêpe batter. If the batter seems too thick, whisk in some of the remaining ¼ cup (2 fl oz/60 ml) milk.

Heat a large nonstick frying pan or crêpe pan over medium-high heat until hot. For each crêpe, pour 2 tablespoons batter into the pan to form a round about 1½ inches (4 cm) in diameter and spaced 1 inch (2.5 cm) apart. Cook until the edges are crisp and golden on the first side, about 3 minutes. Using a spatula, turn the crêpes and cook until golden on the second side, about 2 minutes longer. Transfer to a warmed platter. Repeat with the remaining batter.

To serve, arrange the crêpes on a plate. Spoon a dollop of Crème Fraîche onto each crêpe. Garnish the crêpes with chives and serve at once.

Buckwheat flour is used in the classic crêpe of Brittany, a region also known for butter, cream, and *fleur de sel*. The dark-brown flour produces a sturdier crêpe than white flour, making it ideal to use as a base for a bite-size appetizer. Other suggested toppings are crème fraîche with caviar or chives; soft unsalted butter with shredded Gruyère cheese; crumbled blue cheese; minced ham and cheese; and apple compote.

Pork Pâté

Every part of the pig is used in French cooking, and some of the most delectable dishes have been devised with the less than noble parts, such as the liver and back fat. Seasonings such as juniper, mustard seed, coriander, and fennel play an important part in the final flavor of this terrine, and can vary according to taste and regions, as can the proportion of liver to meat. For easy slicing, use a weight such as a foil-wrapped brick to press out the excess liquid and compress the terrine. Curing salt, which helps to keep the color of the meat fresh looking, can be purchased online; fresh pork liver, pork back fat, and caul fat can be ordered from butcher shops.

Place the liver in a bowl and cover with the milk. Cover and refrigerate overnight.

In a large bowl, combine the back fat, pork shoulder, sea salt, pepper, curing salt, bay leaf, allspice and juniper berries, mustard seeds, paprika, nutmeg, and brandy. Using your hands, mix well to combine. Cover and refrigerate overnight.

Drain the liver and discard the milk. Rinse the liver several times under running cold water and pat dry with paper towels. Cut the liver into 1-inch (2.5-cm) cubes, add to the pork mixture, and mix well to combine.

Place the pork mixture in a food processor and pulse until finely chopped. Return to the large bowl.

In another large bowl, stir together the Chicken Stock, cream, and bread crumbs. Add to the ground meat mixture and, using your hands, mix to combine. Transfer the new mixture to the food processor and pulse until well mixed, 1–2 minutes. It will be a loose and wet mixture.

Preheat the oven to 300°F (150°C). Line a 2-quart (2-l) pâté mold or meat-loaf terrine with the caul fat, allowing it to drape over the ends and sides.

Tightly pack the meat mixture into the prepared mold. Tap the mold on the work surface several times to eliminate any air pockets. Fold the exposed caul fat over the top of the mold to enclose the meat mixture.

Cover the mold and place it in a larger baking dish. Pour boiling water into the larger dish until it reaches halfway up the sides of the mold. Bake until an instant-read thermometer inserted into the center reads 145°F (63°C), about 1 1/2 hours. Add more boiling water during cooking if it evaporates below the halfway mark.

If desired, for a very tight, dense terrine, uncover and, while the terrine is still hot, place a weight on top to press out any excess juices. Let cool to room temperature, cover, and refrigerate for at least 2 days before serving.

To remove the pâté from the pan: Insert a knife along the edges of the pâté to loosen it. Gently warm the bottom of the pan in a little warm water for a few seconds, then place a plate upside down on top of the pan and invert the plate and pan together. Lift off the pan.

To serve, carefully cut into slices about 1/2 inch (12 mm) thick; an unweighted pâté may be a bit crumbly.

1/4 lb (250 g) fresh pork liver

2 cups (16 fl oz/500 ml) whole milk

1/2 lb (500 g) pork back fat, cut into 1/2-inch (12-mm) cubes

2 lb (1 kg) pork shoulder, cut into 1-inch (2.5-cm) cubes

1 tablespoon coarse sea salt

1/2 teaspoon freshly ground pepper

1/4 teaspoon curing salt (see note)

1/2 bay leaf

2 each allspice berries and juniper berries, finely crushed

1/4 teaspoon yellow mustard seeds

1/4 teaspoon sweet Spanish paprika

Pinch of freshly grated nutmeg

1/4 cup (2 fl oz/60 ml) brandy

1/4 cup (2 fl oz/60 ml) Chicken Stock (page 272) or chicken broth

3 cups (24 fl oz/750 ml) heavy (double) cream

2 tablespoons fresh bread crumbs

1 piece caul fat, about 16 inches (40 cm) square (see note)

Boiling water as needed

MAKES 12–14 SERVINGS

Herring Marinated in Olive Oil and Fresh Herbs

1 jar (12 oz/375 g) wine-pickled snack herring

2–3 tablespoons extra-virgin olive oil, plus extra

2 tablespoons minced mixed fresh chives, Italian (flat-leaf) parsley, and tarragon

8 heads white or red Belgian endive (chicory/witloof)

3 tablespoons pink peppercorns

MAKES 10–12 SERVINGS

Drain the herring, rinse under running cold water, drain again, and pat dry with paper towels. Using a sharp knife, cut the herring into small cubes.

In a bowl, combine the herring, 2 tablespoons of the olive oil, and the mixed herbs and toss to coat, adding more olive oil if needed.

Trim 1/2 inch (12 mm) from the stem end of each endive head and separate the leaves. Arrange 40 of the largest leaves on a large platter; reserve the smaller leaves for another use or discard.

Spoon a dollop of the herring mixture onto the base of each leaf, covering about one-third of the surface. Top with 2 or 3 peppercorns and serve at once.

Herring is popular throughout the coastal regions of France and is served primarily as an hors d'oeuvre and in salads. The pieces of pickled fish are combined with crème fraîche or with olive oil and fresh herbs as in this recipe. The herring can also be served on leaves of radicchio, thin slices of cucumber, or crackers.

Les Entrées

About Les Entrées

Adapted into the English language, the word *entrée* has evolved to refer to the main course. In France, it is literally the "entrance" to a meal, setting the stage for the centerpiece, or *le plat*. The portions are not large, but the flavors are vibrant, and the choices varied.

Garden-fresh vegetables figure prominently in many first courses, especially vegetable soups and composed salads.

At the beginning of just about any meal, French cooks often start with a vegetable soup that is sometimes enriched with cream or milk. These simple soups rely on seasonal, fresh ingredients to give them outstanding flavor. Fava Bean Soup (page 86) brings out the herbal nuances and smooth texture of this favorite springtime legume. The sweetness of summer tomatoes shines through in an elegant tomato soup topped with a delicate crust of puff pastry (page 80). Cauliflower Soup with Chervil (page 79) and Cream of Chestnut Soup (page 85), both creamy purées, are delicious and satisfying ways to savor wintertime ingredients.

The same emphasis on freshness also applies to salads. At the French table, salads can appear before or after the main course. Beet and Mâche Salad with Citrus Dressing (page 93) and Salade Verte (page 94), which bathes peppery arugula (rocket) leaves in a dressing of balsamic and Champagne vinegars combined with olive oil, are a welcome refreshment after a rich main course and a palate cleanser before upcoming cheese and dessert courses. French salads are also a platform for creating interesting contrasts of texture and temperature. Fried goat cheese rounds, sautéed chanterelle mushrooms, roasted pork tenderloin, and poached eggs are four typical examples of warm ingredients used to mix into a bed of fresh greens.

INTERESTING EGGS

Outside of France, eggs are often regarded as a breakfast food. In French cooking, they play many roles. Traditionally, eggs were an excellent and easily available source of nutrition for people who lived on farms, and over the years, rural French cooks have developed creative and delicious ways to serve them. Now, it is customary for an egg dish to make an appearance as a first course, especially at dinnertime.

In Burgundy, where the regional specialty, Pinot Noir, goes into innumerable dishes and sauces, poached eggs are presented on a pool of luscious red wine and tomato sauce (page 102) and accompanied with toast as a first course. In the Périgord and Gascony, the aromatic truffle makes its way into scrambled eggs (page 112), which are prepared so carefully that they slowly thicken into a silken mass rather than quickly curdling. France is famous for originating the soufflé, a masterpiece of kitchen conjuring that transforms dense, rich eggs into a tall, light, and airy dish. Among the countless flavoring possibilities is a soufflé that incorporates blue cheese and walnuts (page 111).

Quiches and omelettes hold a place of honor at the French table. Quiche, a national favorite, is also among the typical street foods in France. It is easy to find vendors whose carts hold small pies offering a choice of fillings. Two classic versions are offered here, Ham and Leek Quiche (page 107) and Quiche Lorraine (page 108) with bacon and Gruyère cheese, both baked in a butter-rich pastry shell. Once you are comfortable making the pastry, you will discover that the custard filling is a savory blank canvas for a variety of different meats, cheeses, and vegetables. Omelettes are also served as the entrée of a multi-course meal. The one in this chapter (page 106) is filled with Sauce Verte (page 268), a mixture of fresh herbs that perfectly complements the eggs.

Although quiches, omelettes, and other egg dishes are prepared as first courses, they also make excellent light suppers when accompanied with a simple salad. Other entrées, namely a hearty soup with abundant vegetables like Soupe au Pistou (page 83) or French Onion Soup (page 89), can also be paired with a salad for a simple dinner.

SELECTING L'ENTRÉE

A French meal strives for balance. The appreciation of an entrée does not take a secondary position to the enjoyment of a main dish. Rather, each course of a meal is allotted its proper share of attention. The French cook carefully selects the courses to make sure that they complement one another. When a substantial main course is planned, a lighter entrée is called for, and vice versa.

Sometimes, the courses can be of equal weight. Salade Niçoise (page 95), a composed salad of crisp raw vegetables and protein in the form of tuna, olives, hard-boiled eggs, and sometimes anchovies, is satisfying enough that a light seafood main dish such as Scallops in Tangerine Sauce (page 120) will be ample enough to fill out the menu. The philosophy underlying the custom of serving an entrée before a main course is that the portions should be moderate in size, so that diners come away pleasantly sated with the cook's inspired menu combinations.

CENTRE

Cauliflower Soup with Chervil

This is one of the many creamy vegetable soups typical of French home cooking. A vegetable, in this case cauliflower, is cooked with milk or a mixture of cream and milk, seasoned, and puréed, and then garnished with fresh herbs. Sometimes a little potato is added for thickening the soup, as you see here.

Coarsely chop the cauliflower, including the core.

Bring a large saucepan of water to a boil over medium-high heat. Add the chopped cauliflower and diced potato, reduce the heat to medium, and cook until it softens slightly, about 5 minutes. Drain well and return to the pan.

Add 2$\frac{1}{2}$ cups (20 fl oz/625 ml) of the milk and the salt to the cauliflower and bring to a boil over medium-high heat. Reduce the heat to medium, cover, and cook until the cauliflower and potato are easily pierced with a fork, 15–20 minutes.

Working in batches in a blender or food processor, or using an immersion blender, purée the soup until smooth, adding the remaining milk as needed to reach the desired creamy consistency.

Transfer the soup to a clean saucepan over medium heat and bring to a simmer. Stir in the butter, nutmeg, and pepper. Taste and adjust the seasoning with salt.

Transfer the soup to a warmed soup tureen or ladle into individual bowls. Garnish with the chervil and serve at once.

1 small head cauliflower, about $\frac{3}{4}$ lb (375 g)

1 boiling potato, about $\frac{1}{2}$ lb (250 g), peeled and diced

3$\frac{1}{4}$–3$\frac{1}{2}$ cups (26–28 fl oz/ 810–875 ml) whole milk

$\frac{1}{2}$ teaspoon salt

2 tablespoons unsalted butter

$\frac{1}{8}$ teaspoon freshly grated nutmeg

$\frac{1}{4}$ teaspoon freshly ground white pepper

$\frac{1}{4}$ cup ($\frac{1}{3}$ oz/10 g) fresh chervil leaves

MAKES 6 SERVINGS

Tomato Soup with Puff Pastry

2 lb (1 kg) ripe tomatoes, cored

½ cup (4 oz/125 g) unsalted butter

½ yellow onion, chopped

3 cloves garlic, minced

1 bay leaf

2 teaspoons minced fresh thyme

1 teaspoon *each* salt and freshly ground pepper

4 cups (32 fl oz/1 l) heavy (double) cream

All-purpose (plain) flour for dusting

2 sheets puff pastry, thawed if frozen

1 large egg beaten with 2 teaspoons water

MAKES 6 SERVINGS

Bring a saucepan of water to a boil over medium-high heat. Cut an X in the blossom end of each tomato. Using a slotted spoon, lower the tomatoes into the boiling water and cook for 30 seconds. Drain. When cool enough to handle, slip off the skin starting at the X and discard. Quarter the tomatoes and set aside.

In a large saucepan over medium heat, melt the butter. Add the onion and sauté until translucent, 2–3 minutes. Add the garlic and sauté for 1 minute. Reduce the heat to low and add the tomatoes, bay leaf, thyme, salt, and pepper. Cook, stirring, until the tomatoes are soft, about 20 minutes. Discard the bay leaf.

Working in batches in a blender or food processor, or using an immersion blender, purée the tomato mixture until smooth. Strain through a fine-mesh sieve into a bowl; discard the tomato seeds. Return the tomato mixture to the pan, stir in the cream, and bring to a simmer over medium heat. Remove from the heat.

Preheat the oven to 400°F (200°C). On a lightly floured work surface, roll out the puff pastry until ¼ inch (6 mm) thick and use a knife to cut out 6 rounds that are slightly larger than the diameter of an ovenproof soup bowl. Arrange the pastry rounds on a baking sheet and refrigerate for 10 minutes. Place the soup bowls on another baking sheet. Ladle the soup into the bowls, filling them to within ½ inch (12 mm) of the rim. Place a pastry round on top of each bowl and pull the edges tight. Brush the pastry with the egg wash. Bake until the pastry is puffed and golden in color, 12–15 minutes. Serve at once.

The pairing of two French classics such as creamy tomato soup topped with a dome of light golden puff pastry is a modern-day indulgence. Inspired by the French chef Philippe Jeanty, of the famous Bistro Jeanty in California's Napa Valley, this soup is sure to please the guests at your table.

French Onion Soup

Topped with a thick piece of toasted bread and a generous amount of melted Gruyère cheese, onion soup was the favorite early-morning fare of the vendors and buyers who frequented the tiny restaurants surrounding Les Halles, the famous Parisian wholesale produce and meat market. Although the market was torn down in 1971, the soup remains popular in Paris and throughout France.

In a large, heavy saucepan over medium heat, melt the butter with the olive oil. When the butter foams, stir in the onions and sauté until translucent, 4–5 minutes. Reduce the heat to low, cover, and cook until the onions are lightly golden, about 15 minutes. Uncover and sprinkle with the sugar and salt. Raise the heat to medium and cook uncovered, stirring often, until the onions are deep golden brown in color, 30–40 minutes.

Sprinkle the flour over the onions and cook, stirring, until the flour is browned, 2–3 minutes. Stirring constantly, gradually pour in the bouillon and 2 cups (16 fl oz/500 ml) water. Raise the heat to high and bring to a boil. Stir in the wine and the pepper. Reduce the heat to low, cover, and cook until the onions begin to fall apart, about 45 minutes.

Meanwhile, make the topping: Preheat the broiler (grill). Arrange the bread slices in a single layer on a baking sheet. Toast the bread, turning once, until dried out but not browned, 6–8 minutes total. Remove the pan from the oven. Rub both sides of the bread with the garlic halves and brush both sides with the olive oil. Return to the oven, turning once, until golden, 4–6 minutes total. Set aside.

Preheat the oven to 450°F (230°C).

Place 6–8 ovenproof soup bowls on a rimmed baking sheet. Ladle the soup into the bowls, filling them to within 1/2 inch (12 mm) of the rim. Top each with 1 toasted baguette slice, sprinkle evenly with the cheese, and dot with the butter. Bake until a golden crust forms and the soup bubbles around the edges, about 15 minutes. Serve at once.

6 tablespoons (3 oz/90 g) unsalted butter

1 tablespoon extra-virgin olive oil

2 lb (1 kg) yellow onions, very thinly sliced

1/2 teaspoon sugar

1/2 teaspoon salt

1 1/2 teaspoons all-purpose (plain) flour

8 cups (64 fl oz/2 l) Beef Bouillon (page 272) or beef broth

1 cup (8 fl oz/250 ml) dry white wine

1 teaspoon freshly ground pepper

For the topping

6–8 slices coarse country bread, each about 1/2 inch (12 mm) thick

2 cloves garlic, halved

3 tablespoons extra-virgin olive oil

2 cups (8 oz/250 g) shredded Gruyère or Emmentaler cheese

2 tablespoons unsalted butter, cut into small pieces

MAKES 6–8 SERVINGS

Frisée Salad with Poached Egg and Lardons

4 slices thick-cut bacon, cut into ½-inch (12-mm) pieces

3 tablespoons extra-virgin olive oil

1 tablespoon red wine vinegar

¼ teaspoon freshly ground pepper, plus extra for seasoning

Salt

2 heads frisée, pale inner leaves only, rinsed and dried well

4 large eggs

MAKES 4 SERVINGS

Line a large plate with paper towels. In a frying pan over medium-high heat, fry the bacon pieces, turning once or twice, until crisp, 6–7 minutes. Transfer to the paper towels to drain.

In a bowl, whisk together the olive oil, vinegar, pepper, and salt to taste. Tear the frisée leaves into bite-size pieces. Add the frisée and the bacon to the bowl and toss well to coat. Divide the salad among four individual salad plates.

Bring a frying pan with 1 inch (2.5 cm) of water just to a simmer over medium-high heat. Reduce the heat to low. Break an egg into a small bowl and slide the egg into the water. Repeat with the remaining 3 eggs. Gently spoon the simmering water over the eggs and cook until the whites are just opaque and a film forms over the yolks, about 4 minutes.

Using a slotted spatula, carefully transfer each egg to a salad, gently sliding it on top. Season with the ground pepper, and serve at once.

In French markets both large and small, *lardons*, small strips of smoked or unsmoked bacon, are considered convenience food and are found prepackaged in the same section as sliced ham and prosciutto. Used in numerous ways, *lardons* are an essential ingredient in this salad. When broken, the poached egg combines with the vinaigrette to make a creamy dressing that coats the bitter greens, and the *lardons* provide a salty contrast.

Beet and Mâche Salad with Citrus Dressing

Mâche, also known as lamb's lettuce, is a mildly nutty green that grows in delicate rosettes or in long, strappy, clustered leaves. It thrives only in cool temperatures, and thus is a popular winter salad green in France. Combining roasted beets with mâche and a fresh citrus dressing makes a truly seasonal winter salad.

Preheat the oven to 350°F (180°C).

Place the beets in a roasting pan. Drizzle with 1 1/2 tablespoons of the olive oil and toss to coat. Roast, turning once or twice, until easily pierced with a fork, about 45 minutes for small beets and 1–1 1/4 hours for large beets. Remove the roasting pan from the oven.

When the beets are cool enough to handle, slip off the skins and discard. Thinly slice the beets and set aside.

In a bowl, whisk together the remaining 2 1/2 tablespoons olive oil, the lemon juice, orange juice, mustard, salt, and pepper. Add the mâche and toss well to coat.

Divide the mâche among individual salad plates. Add the beets to the bowl and gently turn to coat in the remaining dressing. Divide the beets among the salads, tucking some under and some on top of the mâche.

Sprinkle with the minced parsley and serve at once.

6 small beets or 3 large beets, about 1 lb (500 g) total

4 tablespoons (2 fl oz/60 ml) extra-virgin olive oil

1 tablespoon fresh lemon juice

2 tablespoons fresh orange juice

1/4 teaspoon Dijon mustard

1/2 teaspoon salt

1/4 teaspoon freshly ground white pepper

3 cups (3 oz/90 g) mâche, rinsed and dried well

2 tablespoons fresh minced flat-leaf (Italian) parsley

MAKES 4 SERVINGS

Salade Verte

3 cups (3 oz/90 g) arugula
(rocket) or 1 small head
romaine (cos) lettuce

2 teaspoons *each* Champagne
vinegar and extra-virgin
olive oil

1 teaspoon *each* balsamic
vinegar and Dijon mustard

1 shallot, finely chopped

1 teaspoon minced fresh
tarragon

Salt and freshly ground
pepper

MAKES 4 SERVINGS

If using arugula, remove any large stems. If using romaine, remove the dark outer leaves and save for another use or discard. Trim the base of the head and tear the remaining leaves into several pieces. Rinse the arugula or romaine leaves, dry well with paper towels, and set aside.

In a bowl, combine the Champagne vinegar, olive oil, balsamic vinegar, and mustard. Whisk until blended. Stir in the shallot and tarragon. Season to taste with salt and pepper. Add the arugula or romaine and toss well to coat.

Divide the salad among individual salad plates and serve at once.

This simple green salad composed of fresh greens and a balsamic vinaigrette is usually served after the main course. In Parisian restaurants, it is also presented with the cheese course.

Savoy Salad

¼ lb (125 g) thick-cut bacon

5 cups (5 oz/155 g) escarole
(Batavian endive) leaves

¼ cup (2 fl oz/60 ml)
extra-virgin olive oil

2 tablespoons walnut oil

Salt and freshly ground pepper

¼ lb (125 g) Beaufort cheese,
cut into cubes

¼ cup (1 oz/30 g) coarsely
chopped toasted walnuts

MAKES 4 SERVINGS

Cut the bacon into 1-inch (2.5-cm) pieces. Heat a frying pan over medium heat and add the bacon. Sauté until it is crisp and has rendered its fat, 4–5 minutes. Transfer to paper towels to drain. Separate the pale yellow inner leaves from the escarole and tear into bite-size pieces. Save the remaining leaves for another use or discard. Rinse the escarole and dry well with paper towels.

In a large bowl, combine the olive and walnut oils. Season to taste with salt and pepper. Whisk until blended. Add the escarole leaves and toss well to coat.

Add the bacon, cheese, and walnuts to the bowl and toss well.

Divide the salad among individual salad plates and serve at once.

Walnuts and Beaufort cheese are the pride of the town of Savoy and complement each other well in this composed salad. Other lettuces such as romaine (cos) could be used in place of the escarole.

Salade Niçoise

The word *niçoise*, meaning "from or of Nice," indicates that the dish is full of the flavors of the South of France: olives, capers, tomatoes, anchovies, and tuna. Although it has many versions, salade niçoise typically includes haricots verts, slender, young green beans, along with boiled potatoes, hard-boiled eggs, and lettuce. The most authentic version calls for canned, olive oil–packed tuna, rather than fresh or water-packed tuna.

Trim the stem ends of the haricots verts. Bring a saucepan of water to a boil over medium-high heat. Add the haricots verts and cook until tender, 2–3 minutes. Using a slotted spoon, transfer the beans to a colander and rinse under running cold water. Add the potatoes to the boiling water and cook until tender, 10–12 minutes. Drain and rinse under running cold water until cool enough to handle. Cut the potatoes into chunks.

Separate the leaves from the lettuce. Rinse the leaves and dry well. Cut the tomatoes into quarters. Peel the hard-boiled eggs and cut in half lengthwise. Arrange the lettuce leaves on a large platter. Make small mounds of the haricots verts, potatoes, tomatoes, and tuna on top of the lettuce. Arrange the egg halves around the mounds and scatter the anchovies and olives on top.

Drizzle the salad with the olive oil and vinegar. Sprinkle with the salt and pepper and serve at once.

1 lb (500 g) haricots verts

4 boiling potatoes

1 head butter (Boston) lettuce

4 ripe tomatoes

4 large eggs, hard-boiled (page 275)

1 can (7 oz/220 g) tuna

12 anchovy fillets

1/3 cup (2 oz/60 g) niçoise olives

1/4 cup (2 fl oz/60 ml) extra-virgin olive oil

2 cups (16 fl oz/500 ml) red wine vinegar

1/2 teaspoon *each* sea salt and freshly ground pepper

MAKES 6 SERVINGS

Butter Lettuce with Dijon Vinaigrette

At bistros and cafeterias in France, you'll often find a green salad on the menu. More often than not, it will be leaves of butter lettuce atop several spoonfuls of thick, mustard-laced vinaigrette and served in an individual bowl. The diner tosses the salad at the table, coating the leaves with the thick, tangy dressing.

Separate the heads of lettuce into individual leaves. Tear the larger leaves into several pieces; keep the medium and small leaves whole. You should have 4–5 cups (4–5 oz/125–155 g). Rinse the leaves, dry well, and set aside.

In a large bowl, combine the olive oil and mustard and whisk until thick. Whisk in the vinegar and salt. Add the lettuce leaves and toss well to coat.

Divide the salad among individual salad plates. Serve at once.

1 large or 2 medium heads butter (Boston) lettuce

1/4 cup (2 fl oz/60 ml) extra-virgin olive oil

2 teaspoons Dijon mustard

2 tablespoons red wine vinegar

1/2 teaspoon salt

MAKES 4–6 SERVINGS

Arugula with Fried Goat Cheese

¼ lb (4 oz/125 g) fresh
goat cheese

½ cup (2 oz/60 g) dried
medium-fine bread crumbs

¼ teaspoon sea salt or
kosher salt

½ teaspoon freshly ground
pepper

½ teaspoon fresh thyme
leaves

4 cups (4 oz/125 g) arugula
(rocket) leaves, coarse stems
trimmed, rinsed and drained
well

Classic Vinaigrette
(page 273)

1 tablespoon extra-virgin
olive oil

MAKES 4 SERVINGS

Warm goat cheese is a favorite addition to French salads. Fresh, young, raw goat's milk cheese is often the choice. However, due to regulations regarding raw milk, these cheeses are not available in some countries outside of France. This version of the classic salad uses a fresh pasteurized goat's milk cheese that is shaped into patties, covered lightly with herbed bread crumbs, and fried.

Shape the cheese into 4 equal rounds, each 3 inches (7.5 cm) in diameter and ½ inch (12 mm) thick. If using a log-shaped cheese, cut it into 4 equal slices, each ³⁄₄ inch (2 cm) thick.

In a bowl, stir together the bread crumbs, salt, pepper, and thyme. Spread the mixture on a piece of waxed paper. Working with 1 round of cheese at a time, press both sides into the mixture to coat it. Set aside.

In a large bowl, combine the arugula and the vinaigrette and toss to coat. Divide the salad among individual salad plates and set aside.

In a small frying pan over medium heat, warm the olive oil. Add the cheese rounds and cook until lightly golden, 1–2 minutes. Turn the rounds and cook until the cheese begins to melt and spread slightly, about 1 minute longer. Remove the pan from the heat and set aside.

Using a spatula, quickly transfer each browned cheese round to a salad, gently sliding it on top. Serve at once.

Endive Salad

½ cup (2 oz/60 g) walnuts

3 oz (90 g) blue cheese

3 tablespoons extra-virgin olive oil

2 teaspoons Champagne vinegar

1 small shallot, minced

Freshly ground pepper

6 heads Belgian endive (chicory/witloof)

2 red apples

2 tablespoons minced chives

MAKES 4–6 SERVINGS

Preheat the oven to 350°F (180°C). Spread the walnuts in a single layer on a baking sheet and toast, stirring once, until golden, 8–10 minutes. Set aside.

In a small bowl, combine one-third of the cheese, the olive oil, and the vinegar. Using a fork, mash the cheese into the oil and vinegar to blend. Stir in the shallot and ¼ teaspoon pepper. Set aside.

Rinse and dry the endive well. Cut a ½-inch (12-mm) cone from the stem end of each endive. Coarsely chop 3 of the heads. Slice the remaining head lengthwise into slivers ¼ inch (6 mm) thick. Add the endive to the bowl. Core the apples and cut them lengthwise into slices ½ inch (12 mm) thick. Add to the bowl. Add the walnuts and toss the salad well.

Divide the salad among individual salad plates, arranging the apple slices on top. Crumble the remaining two-thirds cheese and divide among the salads. Sprinkle with the chives and serve at once.

Endive comes in two varieties: the large, lettucelike head that is a relative of frisée and the tight, pointed head, or *chicon*, also known as Belgian endive. These heads have delicate leaves that are white or red and white (choose either for this salad), rather than green, because they have never been exposed to sunlight. The slightly bitter endive is a key element in winter salads like this one.

Greens with Sautéed Mushrooms

Any combination of greens or herbs—such as arugula (rocket), frisée, spinach, or dandelion greens—can be used in this warm salad. With their firm texture and mildly earthy flavor, chanterelles are the ideal complement to the crisp greens, but oyster or shiitake mushrooms make a flavorful substitute.

Clean the mushrooms with a brush. Halve or quarter any large mushrooms; leave the small ones whole. Rinse the greens, dry well, and set aside.

In a small frying pan or sauté pan over medium-high heat, melt the butter with 1 tablespoon of the olive oil. When the butter foams, add the mushrooms, 1/4 teaspoon salt, and sauté until the mushrooms are soft and have released their juices, about 2–3 minutes. Set aside.

In a bowl, whisk together the remaining 2 tablespoons olive oil, the shallots, half of the chives, 3/4 teaspoon salt, 1/2 teaspoon pepper, and the vinegar. Add the greens and toss well to coat.

Divide the salad among individual salad plates. Spoon the warm mushrooms on top. Sprinkle with the remaining chives and serve at once.

1/2 lb (250 g) mushrooms

5 cups (5 oz/155 g) mixed greens

2 teaspoons unsalted butter

3 tablespoons olive oil

Salt and freshly ground pepper

2 teaspoons minced shallots

1 tablespoon minced fresh chives

2 teaspoons red wine vinegar

MAKES 4 SERVINGS

Roasted Pork Tenderloin and Cornichon Salad

This composed salad can be served as a first course on individual plates or family style on a platter. You can increase the amount of ingredients to make the salad substantial enough for lunch or a light supper. Mustard and freshly sliced baguettes commonly accompany the salad, but resist the temptation to construct a sandwich—the French way is to eat the bread alongside.

Preheat the oven to 400°F (200°C).

Sprinkle the tenderloins with the salt and pepper. In an ovenproof frying pan just large enough to hold the tenderloins, melt the butter with 2 teaspoons of the olive oil over medium-high heat. When the butter foams, add the tenderloins and sear, turning once, until browned, about 6 minutes total. Transfer the pan to the oven and roast until an instant-read thermometer inserted into the middle of a tenderloin registers 150°F (65°C), 12–15 minutes. Transfer the tenderloins to a platter and tent with aluminum foil to keep warm.

Separate the head of butter lettuce into leaves; reserve the larger outer leaves for another use. Arrange the smaller, pale yellow inner leaves and the arugula leaves on a platter. Drizzle with the remaining 1 teaspoon olive oil and the vinegar to taste. Cut the tenderloins into slices ½ inch (12 mm) thick.

Arrange the sliced pork and cornichons on top of the greens. Serve at once, accompanied by Dijon mustard.

2 pork tenderloins, each about ¾ lb (375 g)

1 teaspoon *each* salt and freshly ground pepper

1 tablespoon unsalted butter

3 teaspoons extra-virgin olive oil

1 head butter (Boston) lettuce, rinsed and well dried

2 cups (2 oz/60 g) baby arugula (rocket) leaves, rinsed and well dried

1–2 teaspoons white wine vinegar

8–12 cornichons

Dijon mustard for serving

MAKES 4–6 SERVINGS

Poached Eggs in Red Wine Sauce

3 tablespoons extra-virgin olive oil

2 yellow onions, coarsely chopped

3 tablespoons all-purpose (plain) flour

1 bottle (24 fl oz/750 ml) red wine such as Pinot Noir

1 lb (500 g) tomatoes, coarsely chopped, or 1 cup (6 oz/185 g) chopped canned plum (Roma) tomatoes with juice

1 Bouquet Garni (page 273)

1 teaspoon salt

1/2 teaspoon freshly ground pepper, plus extra for serving

1 tablespoon unsalted butter

8 large eggs

1 tablespoon minced fresh flat-leaf (Italian) parsley

MAKES 4 SERVINGS

In this recipe, a tomato and wine sauce, cooked down to an unctuous thickness, forms a bed for poached eggs. In the south, around the Rhône River delta, the sauce is also a popular accompaniment to poached salt cod. The dish should be served with garlic-rubbed toasts or fresh baguette slices for soaking up the rich sauce.

In a saucepan over medium high heat, warm the olive oil. Add the onions and sauté until translucent, 2–3 minutes. Sprinkle with the flour and stir until slightly browned, about 2 minutes. Gradually pour in the wine, stirring constantly. Add 2 cups (16 fl oz/500 ml) water, the tomatoes with their juice, Bouquet Garni, salt, and pepper. Raise the heat to high and bring to a boil. Reduce the heat to low and simmer, stirring occasionally, until the sauce has reduced by about two-thirds to one-half, about 20 minutes.

Strain the sauce through a fine-mesh sieve into a clean saucepan. Discard the contents of the sieve. Bring to a boil over medium-high heat. Add the butter, reduce the heat to low, and cook, stirring, until the butter is melted. Taste and adjust the seasonings with salt and pepper.

Bring a frying pan with 2 inches (2.5 cm) of water just to a simmer over medium-high heat. Reduce the heat to low. Break an egg into a small bowl and slide the egg into the water. Repeat with 3 of the remaining eggs. Gently spoon the simmering water over the eggs and cook until the whites are just opaque and a film forms on the yolks, about 4 minutes. Using a slotted spoon, transfer the eggs to a plate and keep warm. Repeat to poach the remaining 4 eggs. Trim the ragged egg edges with a knife or kitchen scissors.

Ladle the sauce into individual shallow bowls. Transfer 2 eggs to each bowl, and sprinkle lightly with pepper and the parsley. Serve at once.

Blue Cheese and Walnut Soufflé

Soufflés are often thought of as desserts, but in French cooking, savory soufflés such as cheese or spinach are held in great regard. Here, blue cheese is combined with finely chopped walnuts for a light beginning to a meal.

Position a rack in the center of the oven, and preheat to 375°F (190°C). Coat a 6-cup (1½-qt/1.5-l) soufflé mold with 1 tablespoon of the butter and then dust lightly with flour. Refrigerate for 15 minutes.

In a large saucepan over low heat, melt the remaining 3 tablespoons butter until it foams. Stir in the flour and cook, stirring, for 1 minute. Add the milk, salt, and pepper, raise the heat to medium, and bring to a boil, whisking constantly. Reduce the heat to low and cook, whisking constantly, for 1 minute. Remove from the heat and whisk in the 4 egg yolks, cheese, and walnuts. Set aside.

In a clean stainless-steel bowl, using a whisk, vigorously beat the 7 egg whites and the cream of tartar until stiff peaks form. Using a rubber spatula, gently fold one-third of the egg whites into the cheese mixture to lighten it, then quickly fold the lightened mixture into the egg whites.

Quickly pour the mixture into the soufflé mold and place on a baking sheet. Bake until puffy and golden and a toothpick inserted in the center comes out clean, about 30 minutes. Serve at once.

4 tablespoons (2 oz/60 g) unsalted butter

¼ cup (1½ oz/45 g) all-purpose (plain) flour

1 cup (8 fl oz/250 ml) whole milk

1 teaspoon salt

½ teaspoon freshly ground pepper

4 large eggs, separated, plus 3 large egg whites, at room temperature

1 cup (5 oz/155 g) crumbled blue cheese

¼ cup (1 oz/30 g) finely chopped walnuts

¼ teaspoon cream of tartar

MAKES 6–8 SERVINGS

Scrambled Eggs with Truffles

4 thin slices *pan de mie* or other white bread

½ cup (4 oz/125 g) unsalted butter, cut into 1-inch (2.5-cm) pieces, plus extra for spreading

8 large eggs

½ oz (15 g) black truffles, finely shaved, plus extra for garnish

½–1 teaspoon salt

½ teaspoon freshly ground pepper

MAKES 4 SERVINGS

Toast the bread in a toaster or preheat the oven to 375°F (190°C). If toasting in the oven, arrange the bread slices in a single layer on a rimmed baking sheet. Bake until lightly golden on the first side, about 8 minutes. Turn and bake until golden on the second side, about 6 minutes longer. Remove the pan from the oven. Spread each slice lightly with butter, cut in half on the diagonal, and set aside.

In a heatproof bowl, whisk together the eggs and shaved truffles until blended. Place the bowl over (not touching) barely simmering water. Add the ½ cup butter and whisk continuously until the eggs thicken into a creamy mass of tiny curds, about 15 minutes. Whisk in the salt and pepper.

Divide the eggs among individual warmed plates. Garnish with the truffle shavings. Serve at once, accompanied with the buttered toast slices.

This is the king of all French egg dishes. French black truffles are in season only from late November through early February. They are called *les truffes noires du Périgord,* "black Périgord truffles." Exuding an earthy, yet sweet aroma unlike anything else, truffles are best savored in simple dishes where they are warmed just enough to maximize their fragrance and flavor.

Les Plats

About Les Plats

At the centerpiece of the table is a main course of meat, poultry, or seafood. Whether *le plat* is a simple sauté, a rustic stew, or a large roast, it does not dominate the menu but is chosen to be in balance with the courses served before and after it.

Meat, especially game, has always commanded respect on the French table, but it was never plentiful for people who were not members of the aristocracy. Indeed, some of the preparations for meat and poultry that are closest to the French heart—braises, stews, and pot-au-feu—are of decidedly peasant origin. These dishes, exemplified by slowly cooked coq au vin and beef brisket, were devised as ways to make tough and inexpensive cuts of meat tender and appealing. Various meats for braising and stewing came from the most well-exercised and muscular parts of the animal, not the tender rib or loin.

Coq au vin was traditionally prepared with an old rooster. Today's cooks make Coq au Vin (page 143) using a chicken from the market rather than a rooster from the farm yard, but they still slowly simmer the bird until it is infused with the characteristic wine sauce. Slow-Braised Pork with Wild Mushrooms (page 161), another dish that traces its origins to farmhouse cooking, braises pork shoulder in a flavorful liquid and tops it with sautéed mushrooms before serving. Similarly, beef brisket (page 158) simmers until it is tender enough to be cut with a fork and is accompanied with Sauce Gribiche (page 270), a piquant combination of cornichons and herbs. Pot-au-Feu (page 164), a hearty preparation of meat and root vegetables, is a legacy from the days when a big pot was kept simmering over a fire fed with the debris from the farm, and odds and ends of meat and vegetables were continually added to the pot. These humble dishes have become part of the

French collective unconscious to the extent that even today animals are butchered in France in a way that is designed to create good cuts for braising (as opposed to the English method of butchering, for example, which aims to offer good cuts for roasting).

Despite the popularity of braises, many main dishes characteristic of today's French cooking are much quicker to prepare. For Steak au Poivre (page 154), boneless rib-eye steaks coated in cracked pepper are briefly seared. After the steaks are removed from the pan, an accompanying sauce is made in the same pan, to take advantage of the savory bits left behind. Other quick-cooking main courses employ a quintessentially French technique: sautéing. Sautéed Chicken with Tomatoes, Bell Peppers, and Olives (page 139) combines ingredients and flavors characteristic of southern France. For Shrimp Sautéed in Butter Sauce (page 123), the shrimp (prawns), cooked in butter and garlic, only take just a few minutes to cook.

The Mediterranean Sea and the Atlantic Ocean, bordering France's extensive coastline, yield countless other varieties of fish and shellfish for main courses. Bouillabaisse (page 133) has regional variants in every coastal area and even in Paris. This chapter's version combines two styles of this classic seafood stew, both with roots in Provence. Bourride (page 137), another Provençal fish soup, poaches fish fillets in a stock that is then enriched with aioli, the region's famous garlic mayonnaise. Salmon fillets are sealed

in parchment (baking) paper packages with simple seasonings of salt, pepper, and lemon slices for cooking en papillote (page 128), a method that at once flavors the fish and preserves its moisture. France's rivers are the source of trout, whose delicate flesh needs nothing more than panfrying and accompanying with a brown butter sauce (page 131).

SELECTING LE PLAT

When deciding on a main course, keep in mind the overall menu and the time of year. In warm-weather months, sautéed foods come together quickly and do not overheat the kitchen. Also appealing is lighter fare as simple as Pan Bagnat (page 127), sandwiches with tuna, sweet peppers, and anchovies. As the days grow shorter and the weather turns chilly, hearty main dishes belong on the menu, such as Baked Halibut with Fennel and Beurre Blanc (page 138), Duck with Cherry Sauce (page 146), and Roast Leg of Lamb with Herbes de Provence and Potatoes (page 167). To precede a rich and substantial main dish, choose a lighter entrée such as a fluffy Blue Cheese and Walnut Soufflé (page 111). Or, follow it with a salad such as Greens with Sautéed Mushrooms (page 99).

For entertaining guests, keep in mind that a sautéed main course requires last-minute preparation, so some of the other courses and offerings—the vegetable accompaniment, hors d'oeuvre, *entrée,* and dessert—can be dishes that you can make ahead. For this reason, soups are excellent *entrées* for serving to company. On the other hand, selecting a long-simmered stew as the main course allows time to prepare an *entrée* or a vegetable side dish that requires last-minute attention before it is presented at the table, leaving the hosts plenty of time to enjoy their guests.

Mussels Steamed in Wine

Moules marinières, or mussels in white wine, is a common waterfront dish in France from the coast of Normandy to St. Tropez. They are often served with French fries, a combination called *moules-frites*. Raised on the dish, locals disdain using forks to loosen the mussels from the shells. Instead, they employ a still-hinged pair of shells as both tongs and eating utensil. Be careful to not overcook the mussels, or they will be tough rather than tender and succulent.

To clean and debeard the mussels, first scrub the shells with a stiff-bristled brush under running cold water. Using a small knife or scissors, cut off the beard, the fibrous tuft at the edge of the shell.

To make the broth, in a large soup pot over medium-high heat, melt the butter with the olive oil. When the butter foams, add the onion and sauté until translucent, 2–3 minutes. Add the mussels, discarding any that fail to close to the touch. Add the wine, thyme, and garlic. Reduce the heat to low, cover, and cook just until the mussels open, 10–12 minutes.

Ladle the mussels along with some broth into individual bowls, discarding any mussels that failed to open. Serve at once.

2½ lb (1.5 kg) mussels

1 tablespoon unsalted butter

1 tablespoon extra-virgin olive oil

½ yellow onion, chopped

1 cup (8 fl oz/250 ml) dry white wine or red wine

1 teaspoon fresh thyme leaves

3 cloves garlic, finely chopped

MAKES 4 SERVINGS

Scallops in Tangerine Sauce

12 sea scallops, about 1½ lb/ 750 g total weight

¼ cup (1 oz/30 g) cornstarch (cornflour)

1 teaspoon salt

½ teaspoon freshly ground pepper

2 tablespoons unsalted butter

2 teaspoons extra-virgin olive oil

1 tablespoon fresh tangerine juice

4 tablespoons (2 fl oz/60 ml) dry white wine, such as Sauvignon Blanc or Muscadet

Frisée or other greens (optional)

MAKES 3 OR 4 SERVINGS

Pat the scallops dry with paper towels. On a large plate, combine the cornstarch, salt, and pepper. Lightly coat the scallops all over with the cornstarch mixture, shaking off the excess.

In a frying pan over medium-high heat, melt ½ tablespoon of the butter with the olive oil. When the butter foams, add the scallops and cook, turning once, until seared on both sides, about 4 minutes total. Add the tangerine juice and 2 tablespoons of the wine and deglaze the pan, scraping the bottom with a wooden spoon to dislodge any browned bits. Reduce the heat to low, add 3 tablespoons water, cover, and cook until the scallops are just opaque, 2–3 minutes. Transfer to a plate and loosely cover with aluminum foil.

Raise the heat to high, add the remaining 2 tablespoons wine to the pan, and deglaze again, scraping the bottom to dislodge any browned bits. Cook until the wine is reduced to about 3 tablespoons, about 2 minutes. Add the remaining 1½ tablespoons butter and stir until it has melted, about 2 minutes.

Divide the scallops and frisée or other greens, if using, among warmed individual plates. Drizzle with the tangerine sauce, and serve at once.

In France, scallops are sold still attached to their fan-shaped, ridged shells. Sometimes the females will have bright orange sacks of roe, which is considered an added delicacy. This preparation is a lighter alternative to the famed cream-based scallop dish, *coquilles St. Jacques*. Here, a simple wine sauce enhances the sweet and slightly nutty flavor of the shellfish without overwhelming it.

Shrimp Sautéed in Butter Sauce

Sautéed shrimp are appreciated all over France, where most towns and even small villages have a fishmonger with excellent quality fish and shellfish. Bright pink from a quick sauté, shrimp are often enhanced by a butter sauce, that is simply made right in the pan. Serve with plenty of bread to soak up the sauce, Butter Lettuce with Dijon Vinaigrette (page 95), and a crisp white wine.

To peel and devein the shrimp, carefully pull off the legs on the inside curve of each shrimp. Peel off the shell, beginning at the head end of the shrimp, pulling off the tail. Using a small knife, carefully cut a shallow groove along the back of each shrimp. With the tip of the knife, gently lift and scrape away the dark vein, then rinse the shrimp under running cold water. Drain on paper towels.

In a frying pan or sauté pan over medium-high heat, melt the butter until it foams. Add the shrimp, sprinkle with the salt and pepper, and cook, turning often, until the shrimp turn pink, about 1 minute. Sprinkle with the garlic and parsley and turn to coat the shrimp well in the sauce.

Transfer the shrimp and sauce to a serving bowl and serve at once.

1 lb (500 g) shrimp (prawns)

4 tablespoons unsalted butter

¼ teaspoon salt

¼ teaspoon freshly ground pepper

1 clove garlic, minced

2 tablespoons minced fresh flat-leaf (Italian) parsley

MAKES 2 OR 3 SERVINGS

Seared Tuna with Pipérade

For the pipérade

2 tablespoons extra-virgin olive oil

1 large yellow onion, minced

1½ *each* green bell peppers and red bell peppers (capsicums), seeded and cut lengthwise into strips ¼ inch (6 mm) wide

6 tomatoes, about 3 lb (1.5 kg) total weight, seeded and chopped

1 clove garlic, minced

½ teaspoon ground *piment d'Espelette* or sweet Spanish paprika

¼ teaspoon ground cayenne pepper

½ teaspoon sugar

½ teaspoon coarse salt

¼ teaspoon freshly ground black pepper

¼ teaspoon coarse salt

4 tuna steaks, each about ⅓ lb (155 g) and about ¾ inch (2 cm) thick

¼ teaspoon freshly ground black pepper

MAKES 4 SERVINGS

To make the *pipérade,* in a frying pan over medium heat, warm the olive oil. Add the onion and sauté until translucent, 2–3 minutes. Add the green and red bell peppers and sauté until they begin to change color and become slightly limp, 3–4 minutes. Cover and cook until very soft and limp, 3–4 minutes longer. Stir in the tomatoes, garlic, *piment d'Espelette*, cayenne, sugar, salt, and black pepper. Reduce the heat to low, cover, and cook until the liquid starts to thicken, 20–25 minutes. Taste and adjust the seasoning.

Choose a frying pan large enough to hold the tuna steaks in a single layer. Place the pan over high heat and sprinkle the bottom evenly with the ¼ teaspoon salt. When the salt is hot, add the tuna and sear on the first side, about 2 minutes. Sprinkle with the black pepper, turn the steaks, and cook until seared on the second side, about 2 minutes longer. Be careful to not overcook; the steaks should be pink in the center.

Transfer the tuna to warmed individual plates or a warmed platter, spoon the *pipérade* over the top, and serve at once.

Pipérade, a sauce of sweet peppers, tomatoes, herbs, and ground *piment d'Espellete,* belongs to the rich cuisine of France's Basque country, located along the border with Spain. Pipérade is also the name given to a dish in which eggs are scrambled into the sauce. *Piments d'Espelletes* are long, slender peppers grown around the town of Espelette. In fall, the buildings of the town are festooned with drying chiles that are later ground to make the spice that finds its way into many dishes of the region. The spice has a haunting, lightly smoky, slightly hot, and somewhat earthy flavor.

Pan Bagnat

The food stalls in the streets of Nice sell this signature sandwich wrapped and ready to eat. The round roll is crunchy on the outside, and its soft interior is liberally sprinkled with olive oil and vinegar, then stacked high with oil-packed tuna, tomatoes, hard-boiled eggs, anchovies, and lettuce. It is perfect picnic or patio fare, no matter where you are.

Using a serrated knife, halve the rolls horizontally. Drizzle the cut sides of the rolls with the olive oil and vinegar.

Cut the bell pepper in half and remove the stem and seeds. Cut the flesh into thin slices. Cut the tomatoes into thin slices. Peel the hard-boiled eggs and then cut the eggs crosswise into thin slices.

In a bowl, using a fork, flake the tuna into small pieces.

Place 1 or 2 lettuce leaves on each of the bottom halves of the rolls. Divide the tuna, bell pepper, tomatoes, eggs, and anchovy fillets evenly among the rolls on top of the lettuce.

Place the top halves of the rolls on the filling and serve at once.

4 large, round, chewy rolls

½ cup (4 fl oz/125 ml) extra-virgin olive oil

2 tablespoons red wine vinegar

1 green bell pepper (capsicum)

2 tomatoes

2 hard-boiled eggs (page 275)

4 oz (125 g) water- or oil-packed tuna, drained

12 anchovy fillets

4–8 delicate lettuce leaves such as butter (Boston), red leaf, or green leaf

MAKES 4 SERVINGS

Salmon en Papillote with Sauce Béarnaise

2 teaspoons unsalted butter plus 1 tablespoon

4 salmon fillets, ¼–⅓ lb (125–155 g) each

Salt and freshly ground pepper

4 thin slices lemon

1 cup (8 fl oz/250 ml) Sauce Béarnaise (page 269)

MAKES 4 SERVINGS

Preheat the oven to 375°F (190°C).

Cut parchment (baking) paper into four 8-by-11-inch (21-by-28-cm) rectangles. Fold the rectangles in half lengthwise and cut each into a heart shape. Lay the hearts flat and coat the inside of the paper with the 1 tablespoon butter.

Place the prepared parchment hearts on a rimmed baking sheet. Arrange a salmon fillet on one half of each heart. Sprinkle the fish lightly with salt and pepper, dot with ½ teaspoon of the remaining butter, and top with a lemon slice. Fold the paper over and press the edges together. Starting from the top of the heart, fold the edges over twice, working your way along the paper's edge to end with a twist at the bottom of the heart (tuck the twist underneath the packet). Repeat to make 3 more packages. Place the packages on a baking sheet.

Bake until the parchment is puffed and starting to darken, 10–16 minutes.

Transfer the parchment packets to individual plates and serve at once, accompanied by the Sauce Béarnaise.

Cooking *en papillote*, literally "in a package," is a classic French way to treat fish, shellfish, and vegetables. The technique not only keeps ingredients from drying out during cooking, but also requires only a small amount of butter or oil, because the ingredients steam within the package. Perfumed with herbs such as tarragon and chervil, Sauce Béarnaise is a classic sauce for fish, and is the perfect choice to enhance these steamed salmon fillets. Sauce Nantua (page 268) also pairs well with salmon.

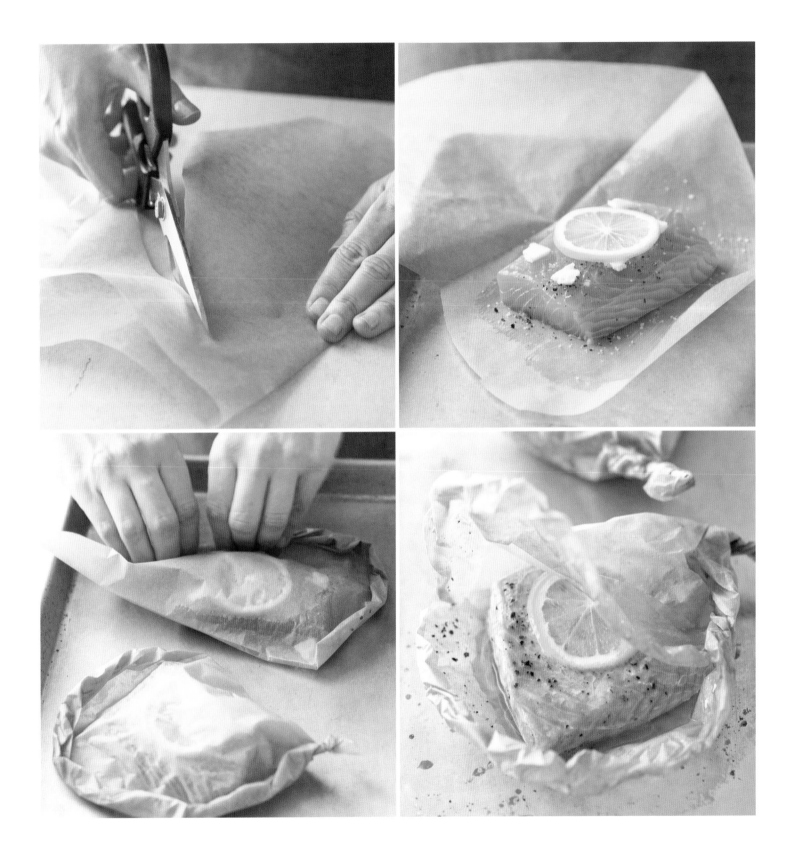

Coq au Vin

One of the iconic dishes of France, coq au vin has its roots in the farmhouse cooking of Burgundy. It was originally made with the tough *coq*, or "rooster," when he was past his prime. Long, slow cooking in wine was required to produce tender meat, and the wine of choice was a red Burgundy. Today, younger chickens are used, and a lighter Pinot Noir from elsewhere could be used and still remain true to the regional flavor of the recipe.

Place the bacon strips in a small saucepan with cold water to cover and bring to a boil over medium-high heat. Reduce the heat to low and simmer for 10 minutes. Drain the bacon, rinse under running cold water, and pat dry with paper towels.

Bring a small saucepan of water to a boil over medium-high heat. Add the pearl onions and boil for 10 minutes. Drain. Cut off the root ends of the onions, slip off the skins, and trim off the stems.

In a deep, large heavy saucepan over medium heat, melt 3 tablespoons of the butter until it foams. Reduce the heat to medium-low, add the bacon and onions, and cook, stirring, until lightly browned, about 10 minutes. Using a slotted spoon, transfer the bacon and onions to a plate. Add the chicken to the pan, raise the heat to medium, and cook, turning as needed, until the chicken begins to brown, about 10 minutes. Sprinkle with the flour and cook, turning occasionally, until the chicken and the flour are browned, about 5 minutes.

Remove the saucepan from the heat and pour the brandy over the chicken. Using a long-handled match, ignite the brandy and let burn until the flames subside. Return the bacon and onions to the pan and place over medium heat. Add 1 cup (8 fl oz/250 ml) of the wine and deglaze the pan, scraping the bottom with a wooden spoon to dislodge any browned bits. Add the remaining $3/4$ cup wine, the thyme, parsley, bay leaf, pepper, and salt, cover, and cook, stirring occasionally, until the chicken is opaque throughout and the meat begins to pull away from the bones, 45–60 minutes.

Meanwhile, in a frying pan over medium-high heat, melt the remaining 1 tablespoon butter until it foams. Add the mushrooms and sauté just until lightly golden, 3–4 minutes. Remove from the heat and set aside. About 15 minutes before the chicken is done, add the mushrooms to the chicken.

Using a slotted spoon, transfer the chicken, onions, mushrooms, and bacon to a bowl. Using a spoon, skim off the fat from the pan juices. Raise the heat to high, bring to a boil, and cook until the liquid has thickened and reduced by nearly half, about 5 minutes. Return the chicken, onions, mushrooms, and bacon to the pan. Reduce the heat to low and cook, stirring, until heated through, 3–4 minutes.

Serve the coq au vin directly from the pan or transfer to a warmed serving dish.

3 oz (90 g) lean bacon, cut into strips 1 inch (2.5 cm) wide and $1/4$ inch (3 mm) thick

12 pearl onions

4 tablespoons (2 oz/60 g) unsalted butter

1 chicken, 4–5 lb (2–2.5 kg), cut into serving pieces

1 tablespoon all-purpose (plain) flour

2 tablespoons brandy

$1^3/4$ cups (14 fl oz/430 ml) red Burgundy or other medium-bodied red wine

3 sprigs fresh thyme

3 sprigs fresh flat-leaf (Italian) parsley

1 bay leaf

1 teaspoon freshly ground pepper

$1/2$ teaspoon salt

$1/2$ lb (250 g) white mushrooms, brushed clean and cut in half

MAKES 4 OR 5 SERVINGS

Cassoulet

For the beans

2 cups (14 oz/440 g) dried white beans such as Great Northern or navy

1 teaspoon salt

1/2 lb (250 g) pork belly

2 carrots, peeled and halved

1 stalk celery, halved

1 yellow onion, studded with 2 whole cloves

1 bay leaf

1 Bouquet Garni (page 273)

2 tablespoons duck or goose fat, or unsalted butter

1 yellow onion, chopped

4 cloves garlic, minced, plus 1 clove, halved

1 cup (6 oz/185 g) chopped canned plum (Roma) tomatoes with juice

1 Bouquet Garni (page 273)

1/2 teaspoon salt

1/2 teaspoon freshly ground pepper

4 legs Duck Confit (page 273)

1 cup (4 oz/125 g) fresh bread crumbs

MAKES 4–6 SERVINGS

To make the beans, pick over the dried beans and discard any misshapen beans or stones, then rinse under running cold water and drain. In a large pot over medium-high heat, combine the beans and 8 cups (64 fl oz/2 l) cold water; discard any beans that float. Add the salt, pork belly, carrots, celery, onion, bay leaf, and Bouquet Garni and cook until the beans are tender, 1 1/2–2 hours. Set aside.

In a frying pan over medium-high heat, warm the duck fat. Add the onion and sauté until translucent, 1–2 minutes. Add the minced garlic and sauté for 1 minute longer. Add the tomatoes and their juice, Bouquet Garni, salt, pepper, and about 1/2 cup (4 fl oz/125 ml) of the bean-cooking broth. Reduce the heat to low, cover, and simmer until the flavors are blended, about 15 minutes.

Remove all of the meat from the duck legs and add it to the mixture. Remove the pork belly from the beans, cut into 1/2-inch (12-mm) cubes, and add to the tomato mixture. Mix well.

Preheat the oven to 325°F (165°C).

To assemble the cassoulet, rub a 4–5-qt (4–5-l) large Dutch oven or other heavy ovenproof pot with the garlic clove. Remove the vegetables, bay leaf, and Bouquet Garni from the beans and discard. Using a slotted spoon, transfer half of the beans to the pot and spread in an even layer. Spoon the duck mixture in a layer over the beans. Top with another layer of the beans and pour about 1/2 cup (4 fl oz/125 ml) of the bean cooking broth over the top. Place on the stove top over medium-high heat and bring to a boil.

Sprinkle the cassoulet with about one-fourth of the bread crumbs, cover, and bake until the crumbs are lightly browned, about 1 hour. Using a spoon, break up the crust and sprinkle with another one-fourth of the bread crumbs. Repeat twice, pouring some of the reserved bean broth over the top if the cassoulet is drying out, and continue to bake until the final layer of bread crumbs is lightly browned, about 1 hour longer; 2 hours total. Remove the cassoulet from the oven and serve at once directly from the pot.

Cassoulet is the pride of many towns in southwestern France, but most especially of Castelnaudary, which is generally agreed upon as the birthplace of this famous crusty bean dish packed with meat. A true cassoulet contains not only the essential duck confit, but also sausages, ham hocks, and perhaps even goose confit and lamb. This is a shortened version of the more complex traditional recipe, but the principle remains the same—as the crust forms, it must be pushed down repeatedly into the beans.

Beef Bourguignon

Beef bourguignon represents French and, more specifically, Burgundian country cooking at its best. A tough, minor cut of beef is transformed into a silken tour de force that can be cut with a fork. The vegetables and the sinews and tendons of the meat, along with the great wine of Burgundy, combine into an unctuous sauce to which mushrooms and pearl onions are added. Serve with steamed or roasted potatoes to soak up the sauce.

Sprinkle the beef cubes with ½ teaspoon of the salt and ¼ teaspoon of the pepper. Spread the flour on a large plate. Lightly coat the cubes with flour, shaking off the excess. Set aside.

Cut the bacon into 1-inch (2.5-cm) pieces. Place the bacon in a saucepan with cold water to cover and bring to a boil over medium-high heat. Reduce the heat to low and simmer for 10 minutes. Drain the bacon, rinse under cold running water, and pat dry with paper towels.

In a Dutch oven or other heavy pot over low heat, warm the olive oil. Add the bacon and cook until crisp and golden, 4–5 minutes. Using a slotted spoon, transfer the bacon to a bowl and set aside. Raise the heat to medium-high and, working in batches, cook the meat, turning as needed, until lightly browned on all sides, about 5 minutes. Transfer to the bowl with the bacon. When all of the meat has been browned, add the carrot and onion and cook until browned, about 5 minutes. Transfer to the bowl with the bacon and meat.

Pour off the fat from the pot. Reduce the heat to medium, add the wine, and deglaze the pot, scraping the bottom with a wooden spoon to dislodge any browned bits. Stir in the beef, bacon, carrot, onion, garlic, thyme, bay leaf, tomato paste, and the remaining ½ teaspoon salt and ¼ teaspoon pepper and bring to a simmer. Reduce the heat to low, cover, and cook until the meat is somewhat tender, about 2½ hours.

Meanwhile, bring a saucepan of water to a boil over medium-high heat. Add the pearl onions and boil for 10 minutes. Drain. Cut off the root ends of the onions, slip off the skins, and trim off the stems. In a frying pan over medium heat, melt the 3 tablespoons butter until it foams. Add the mushrooms and sauté until lightly browned, 4–5 minutes. Using the slotted spoon, transfer the mushrooms to a bowl. Add the pearl onions to the pan and sauté, adding more butter if needed, until golden, about 10 minutes. After the meat has cooked for 2½ hours, add the mushrooms and pearl onions to the pot and continue to cook until the meat is tender enough to cut with a fork, about 1 hour longer.

Using the slotted spoon, transfer the beef, bacon, and vegetables to a bowl. Using a spoon, skim the fat from the surface of the sauce. Raise the heat to medium-high, bring to a boil, and cook until the sauce thickens slightly, 1–2 minutes. Remove from the heat and stir in the beef, bacon, and vegetables. Serve at once in warmed shallow bowls.

3½ lb (1.75 kg) boneless beef chuck roast, or a combination of boneless chuck and beef shank, cut into 2–2½ inch (5–6 cm) cubes

1 teaspoon salt

½ teaspoon freshly ground pepper

All-purpose (plain) flour

6 oz (185 g) bacon

1 tablespoon extra-virgin olive oil

1 carrot, peeled and sliced

1 yellow onion, diced

3 cups (24 fl oz/750 ml) red wine such as Burgundy or Pinot Noir

2 cloves garlic, minced

1 tablespoon fresh thyme leaves, or ½ tablespoon dried thyme

1 bay leaf

1 tablespoon tomato paste

20–24 pearl onions

3 tablespoons unsalted butter, plus extra if needed

1 lb (500 g) mushrooms, brushed clean and thickly sliced

MAKES 6–8 SERVINGS

Steak Frites

Pommes Frites (page 205)

For the steaks

4 rib or rib-eye steaks, each about 6 oz (185 g) and ¹/₂ inch (12 mm) thick

2 tablespoons minced fresh thyme

1 teaspoon freshly ground pepper

1¹/₂ teaspoons coarse salt

MAKES 4 SERVINGS

Steak and French fries, bistro food par excellence, are a favorite everyday meal in France. Children, parents, and grandparents alike find the combination irresistible, but everyone likes the meat cooked just to their liking. *Bleu* is beef that is very, very rare, almost raw; *saignant* is very rare; *a point* is medium rare; and *bien cuit* is well done, though such a request will most likely meet with a medium-well steak. The *frites* must be slender, crisp, well salted, and hot out of the frying oil.

Sprinkle both sides of the steaks with the thyme and pepper. Sprinkle the coarse salt evenly over the bottom of a large frying pan and place over high heat until a drop of water sizzles upon contact, 1–2 minutes. Add the steaks and cook, turning once, until done to your liking, about 4 minutes total for medium rare. Transfer to a warmed platter. Add ¹/₃–¹/₂ cup (3–4 fl oz/80–125 ml) water, as needed, to deglaze the pan, scraping the bottom with a wooden spoon to dislodge any browned bits.

Pour the pan juices over the steaks and serve at once with the hot *frites*.

Beef with Carrots

In this hearty Provençal winter stew, carrots and beef are cooked in local red wine and seasoned with thyme. The sauce should be quite thick; if it is still a bit thin after the meat is tender, remove the meat and carrots and reduce the sauce until it is thick enough to coat the back of a spoon, then return the ingredients to the pot to heat through.

In a Dutch oven or other heavy pot over medium heat, warm the olive oil. Add the onion and garlic and sauté until the onion is nearly translucent, 2–3 minutes. Using a slotted spoon, transfer the onion and garlic to a large plate.

Raise the heat to medium-high. Working in batches, add the beef cubes, a few pieces at a time, and cook, turning as needed, until browned on all sides, about 5 minutes. Using the slotted spoon, transfer the browned meat to the plate with the onion and garlic. When all of the meat has been browned, add 1 cup (8 fl oz/ 250 ml) of the wine and deglaze the pot, scraping the bottom with a wooden spoon to dislodge any browned bits. Add the thyme, bay leaf, salt, pepper, and the remaining 1 cup (8 fl oz/250 ml) wine and stir to combine.

Return the meat, onion, garlic, and any accumulated juices to the pot. Reduce the heat to low, cover, and continue to cook, stirring occasionally, for 1 hour. Add the carrots, cover, and cook, stirring occasionally, until the meat is tender enough to cut with a fork and the sauce has thickened, 1 1/2–2 hours longer. Remove the thyme sprigs and the bay leaf and discard. Taste and adjust the seasonings.

Transfer the stew to a warmed serving bowl or individual bowls. Serve at once.

2 tablespoons extra-virgin olive oil

1 large yellow onion, chopped

3 cloves garlic, chopped

3 lb (1.5 kg) boneless beef chuck, cut into 2-inch (5-cm) cubes

2 cups (16 fl oz/500 ml) dry red wine

4 sprigs fresh thyme

1 bay leaf

1 teaspoon salt

1/2 teaspoon freshly ground pepper

2 lb (1 kg) carrots, peeled and cut into 1-inch (2.5-cm) lengths

MAKES 6 SERVINGS

Beef Brisket with Sauce Gribiche

1 beef brisket, 4–5 lb (2–2.5 kg)

2 teaspoons salt

1 teaspoon freshly ground pepper

1 tablespoon extra-virgin olive oil

2 yellow onions, thinly sliced

2 stalks celery, chopped

1 Bouquet Garni (page 273)

2 cups (16 fl oz/500 ml) dry red wine

2 cups (16 fl oz/500 ml) Beef Bouillon (page 272) or beef broth, plus extra as needed

1 cup (8 fl oz/250 ml) Sauce Gribiche (page 270)

MAKES 4–6 SERVINGS

Preheat the oven to 350°F (180°C).

Rub the brisket all over with the salt and pepper.

In a Dutch oven or other heavy ovenproof pot over medium-high heat, warm the olive oil. Add the brisket and cook, turning once, until well seared on both sides, about 6 minutes total. Transfer to a platter.

Add the onions, celery, and Bouquet Garni to the pot and cook, stirring, until the onions are nearly translucent, about 1 minute. Gradually pour in the wine and deglaze the pot, scraping the bottom with a wooden spoon to dislodge any browned bits. Add the bouillon, return the meat to the pot, and cover. Transfer the pot to the oven and cook until the meat is tender enough to cut with a fork, about 3 hours. Transfer the meat to a carving board and loosely cover with aluminum foil to keep warm.

Using a spoon, skim off the fat from the sauce in the pot. If the sauce is too thick, thin it with a little bouillon or water.

Cut the meat into slices about ½ inch (12 mm) thick and arrange on a warmed platter. Drizzle the braising sauce over the meat or pour it into a warmed bowl and pass at the table. Serve at once, accompanied by the Sauce Gribiche.

Beef brisket is a rich cut of meat and, like other dishes of this kind, is often served with sharply flavored condiments to balance its richness. Here, Sauce Gribiche, made with tart cornichons and herbs, is served alongside.

Pot-au-Feu

1 rump roast, 3–3$\frac{1}{2}$ lb
(1.5–1.75 kg), rolled and tied

2 lb (1 kg) beef shank

2 lb (1 kg) beef short ribs

10 leeks, trimmed

10 carrots, peeled, each cut
into 3 pieces

10 stalks celery, each cut
into 3 pieces

2 yellow onions, each studded
with 2 whole cloves

1 Bouquet Garni (page 273)

Salt and freshly ground
pepper

1 teaspoon peppercorns

4 small turnips, peeled and
quartered

4 parsnips, peeled, halved,
and thick ends quartered

5 large potatoes, about 2$\frac{1}{2}$ lb
(1.25 kg) total weight, peeled
and quartered

8 slices *pain au levain* or
other coarse country bread,
toasted

1$\frac{1}{2}$–2 cups (12–16 fl oz/
375–500 ml) Sauce Verte
(page 268)

Dijon mustard

Cornichons

Coarse sea salt

MAKES 8 SERVINGS

In a large stockpot over high heat, combine the rump roast, beef shank, short ribs, and 6–7 quarts (6–7 l) cold water and bring to a simmer. Simmer, regularly skimming off any scum and froth from the surface with a spoon, until little or no froth remains, about 45 minutes.

Add 3 of the leeks, half of the carrots, half of the celery, the onions, Bouquet Garni, $\frac{1}{2}$ tablespoon salt, and the peppercorns. Partially cover and simmer, skimming occasionally, for about 1$\frac{1}{2}$ hours. Add the remaining leeks, carrots, and celery pieces, the turnips, and the parsnips and simmer until the meat and vegetables are tender, about 1 hour longer.

Meanwhile, place the potatoes in a saucepan with cold water to cover by 2 inches (5 cm) and bring to a boil over medium-high heat. Add 1 teaspoon salt, reduce the heat to medium, and simmer until the potatoes are tender when pierced with a fork, 25–35 minutes. Drain, return to the hot pan, and cover to keep warm.

Using a slotted spoon, transfer the vegetables in the stockpot to a warmed platter and cover loosely with aluminum foil to keep warm. Transfer the meat to another platter and cover to keep warm.

Strain the cooking broth through a fine-mesh sieve into a clean pan. Using a spoon, skim off as much fat from the surface as possible. If there is still a film of fat, gently lay a paper towel on the surface to absorb it; remove and discard the paper towel. Taste and adjust the seasoning with salt and ground pepper. Keep warm.

Remove the strings from the rump roast and discard. Cut the roast across the grain into slices $\frac{1}{2}$ inch (12 mm) thick and arrange on a warmed platter with the other meats. Add the potatoes to the platter and cover to keep warm.

Ladle three-fourths of the broth into warmed bowls and serve accompanied by the toasted bread. Then, ladle the remaining broth over the vegetables and meat and serve accompanied by the Sauce Verte, mustard, cornichons, and coarse sea salt.

Pot-au-feu is part of the French cooking tradition known as *la cuisine grand-mère,* or "grandmother's cooking," which often uses simple ingredients but treats them with great care. The traditional way to serve pot-au-feu is with the meat on one platter, the vegetables on another, and both drizzled with some of the broth and accompanied by a sauce and mustard. The bulk of the broth is reserved for the next day, when pasta is cooked in it, creating yet another nourishing meal. When you purchase the rump roast, ask the butcher to roll and tie it for you. This will help it to cook more evenly.

Sausages and Sauerkraut

Choucroute, or sauerkraut, is a specialty of Alsace in northeastern France, where particular varieties of cabbages, some weighing up to 10 pounds (5 kg), are raised specifically to make the fermented cabbage. Choucroute can be served on its own, but more often it is garnished, in its simplest version with sausages or at its most elaborate with ham hocks, a slab of bacon, and potatoes, as you see here.

Preheat the oven to 325°F (165°C).

If using raw sauerkraut, soak the sauerkraut in a large bowl of cold water for 15 minutes. Taste the sauerkraut and continue to soak if it is too salty. Drain the raw or cooked sauerkraut, place in a kitchen towel, gather up the ends, and wring out any excess water. Place in a bowl and, using a fork, fluff to remove any clumps.

Cut a small square of cheesecloth (muslin). Place the garlic, juniper berries, bay leaf, cloves, and peppercorns in the center, bring the corners together, and tie securely with kitchen twine.

In a Dutch oven or other heavy ovenproof pot over medium heat, warm the lard until melted. Add the onion and sauté slowly, reducing the heat if necessary, until translucent but not browned, about 5 minutes. Add half of the sauerkraut, the cheesecloth bundle, and the ham hocks, and top with the remaining sauerkraut. Add the wine, ground pepper, and water to nearly cover, and bring to a boil.

Cover, transfer to the oven, and cook for 1 hour. Remove from the oven, stir, and add the bacon and the pork belly, if using. Re-cover and cook for 1 hour longer. Remove from the oven, stir, and place the potatoes on top. Recover and cook until the potatoes are tender when pierced with a fork, about 30 minutes longer.

Meanwhile, bring a saucepan full of water to a boil over high heat. Add the sausages, reduce the heat to medium, and cook until hot, 6–8 minutes.

Drain the sauerkraut mixture and turn once or twice. Transfer to a warmed, deep platter and top with the ham hocks and sausages. Cut the bacon and pork belly (if using), into slices and add to the platter with the sauerkraut. Surround the sauerkraut and meat with the potatoes. Serve at once.

3 lb (1.5 kg) raw or cooked sauerkraut

1 clove garlic, minced

10 juniper berries

1 bay leaf

2 whole cloves

6 peppercorns

¼ cup (2 oz/60 g) rendered lard or goose fat

1 large yellow onion, minced

4 smoked ham hocks, about 2 lb (1 kg) total weight

2 cups (16 fl oz/500 ml) dry Riesling, Sylvaner, or other dry white wine

½ teaspoon freshly ground pepper

¼ lb (125 g) slab bacon

¼ lb (125 g) lean pork belly (optional)

8 firm-fleshed potatoes, about 3 lb (1.5 kg) total weight, peeled

6 pork or chicken sausages

MAKES 6–8 SERVINGS

Cheese Fondue

4 or 5 cloves garlic

1 bottle (24 fl oz/750 ml) dry white wine such as Sauvignon Blanc

½ teaspoon salt

1½ lb (750 g) Beaufort or Gruyère cheese, shredded

½ lb (250 g) Comté or Emmentaler cheese, shredded

Pinch of freshly grated nutmeg

¼ cup (2 fl oz/60 ml) kirsch

¼ teaspoon freshly ground pepper

1 tablespoon unsalted butter

Day-old baguettes, cut into 1-inch (2.5-cm) cubes (about 6 cups/³⁄₄ lb/ 375 g total)

2 large eggs

MAKES 4 SERVINGS

Using a garlic press, squeeze the garlic cloves into a fondue pot. Discard the pulp that remains in the press. Pour in the wine and add the salt. Place the pot over medium-high heat and cook the wine mixture just until bubbles begin to appear along the edges of the pot.

Using a wooden spoon, stir in both cheeses. Cook, stirring until the cheeses are nearly melted and the mixture turns yellow, about 10 minutes. Reduce the heat to medium-low and stir in the nutmeg and then the kirsch. Continuing to stir, add the pepper and the butter. Stir until the butter is melted.

To serve, light the fuel burner for the fondue pot according to the manufacturer's instructions. Bring the hot fondue pot to the table and place it over the burner. Put the bread cubes in a bowl or basket and set on the table. Guests spear the bread cubes with a fork, through the crust side so the cubes will stay on better, and then swirl the bread in the fondue. When only a little cheese is left, break the eggs into the pot, stir to combine with the cheese, and cook until crusty. Guests then help themselves to some of the cooked eggs.

The mountain region of Franche-Comté is the source of some of France's most luscious cheeses, which are made from the milk of cows that graze on the region's Alpine pastures. When only a little cheese is left in the fondue pot, eggs are added and cooked to a crusty finish. After diners eagerly scoop up the eggs, a green salad is served.

Raclette

Raclette is both the name of a cow's milk cheese and a dish made with the cheese. Traditionally, chunks of the cheese were put on the hearth near a glowing fire. Diners gathered around, with plates, knives, and forks in hand, and a bowl of boiled potatoes. As the surface of the cheese melted, it was eagerly scraped off, spread across the potatoes, consumed, and enjoyed with wine. Raclette is now popular all over France. If you have a raclette grill, use it for this recipe and follow the manufacturer's instructions.

In a large saucepan, combine the potatoes, the salt, and water to cover. Bring to a boil over medium-high heat, reduce the heat to medium, and cook, uncovered, until the potatoes are easily pierced with a sharp knife, 20–25 minutes. Drain, cover to keep warm, and set aside.

Preheat the oven to 400°F (200°C).

Cut the cheese into slices about 1/2 inch (12 mm) thick and remove the rind. Arrange 1 slice on each of 4 individual heatproof plates. Place the plates in the oven and melt the cheese, 5–7 minutes.

Meanwhile, transfer the potatoes to a serving bowl and arrange the cornichons and bread slices on a plate. Remove the plates of melted cheese from the oven and serve at once. Have each guest spread the cheese on the bread and accompany with the potatoes and cornichons.

12 boiling potatoes, such as Yukon gold, Yellow Finn, or Red or White Rose

1 teaspoon salt

1–1½ lb (500–750 g) raclette cheese

Freshly ground pepper

16 cornichons

Coarse country bread, thinly sliced

MAKES 4 SERVINGS

Les Légumes

About Les Légumes

French gastronomy may be celebrated for its rich meat dishes and cream sauces, but vegetables from spring peas to dried légumes hold a place of honor. In French country cuisine especially, vegetables are cooked simply, to bring out their inherent flavors and textures.

It's easy to be enthusiastic about fresh produce when visiting an open-air market in France where vegetables are treated with the same care and respect given to all other foods. In keeping with the gorgeous visual display that is a key element to the French table, the vegetable and fruit vendors carefully arrange their colorful offerings to catch the eye and lure shoppers, who then pick out the exact specimens that they need for their meals.

To many busy cooks outside of France, a daily trip to the vegetable market, or *marché*, might seem excessive. To French cooks, however, shopping frequently is a necessity, a way of life, and guarantees that they will have the freshest produce for the table.

Even more highly rated by French cooks are vegetables grown in and picked from their own *potager*, or year-round kitchen garden. Serving guests homegrown vegetables is a point of pride to a French host, as is presenting home-cured charcuterie or homemade wine. Any household with a bit of garden space plants a selection of vegetables, fruits, and herbs just a few steps from the kitchen door, from spring fava (broad) beans and summer tomatoes to autumn leeks and winter greens. In addition, the art of foraging is still a common practice in France, and neighbors make a gleeful competition of finding and showing off the first wild mushrooms of autumn or the tiny, red strawberries of spring.

Throughout France, each region boasts its own vegetable specialties. Brittany and Normandy are famed for their large globe artichokes. In the south, the Provençal grow a smaller purple-hued version called the *violette*. The sun-drenched south is also known for shelling beans, sweet peppers (capsicums), and eggplants (aubergines). Chestnuts thrive on the island of Corsica, and cabbages are the pride of the eastern border region of Alsace, as is Belgian endive (chicory/witloof) in the north.

SEASONAL LÉGUMES

In French homes, it's not uncommon to find the main dish accompanied by two garden-fresh vegetable dishes, perhaps a gratin or tian followed by a composed salad, both highlighting the ingredients of the season. Dessert is sometimes replaced with ripe, fresh fruit. When choosing side dishes to accompany main courses, consider which vegetables are in season and how the vegetables might complement or contrast with the main course.

The French make a habit of celebrating each new vegetable as it comes into its peak of ripeness, sometimes enjoying it every day if it has a relatively short season. This has the effect of linking each season with its special offerings in the French mind. Spring arrivals include asparagus, peas, and fava (broad) beans. Summer is the season for tomatoes, eggplants (aubergines), bell peppers (capsicums), and zucchini (courgettes). Autumn brings leeks, fennel, potatoes, and squash such as butternut. Winter is the time for chestnuts, broccoli, and greens such as chard and kale. Artichokes and mushrooms each have two distinct seasons in the spring and autumn.

PLANNING LES LÉGUMES

As a general rule, the heavier and richer the main course, the crisper and brighter the vegetable side dish should be. For example, aromatics such as fennel and leek make especially good companions to rich fish and seafood dishes. Braised Fennel with Raisins and Saffron (page 185), with its licorice-like anise flavor, would make a lively side dish to autumnal Sea Bass with Artichokes (page 134). Similarly, a rich dish like Salmon en Papillote with Sauce Béarnaise (page 128) calls for the contrasting fresh flavors of Spring Peas with Romaine and Mint (page 194) or tender-crisp Sautéed Haricots Verts (page 180). Sometimes a complementary vegetable is better than a contrasting one: Chard Gratin (page 187) transforms a crisp, somewhat bitter wintry green into a more hearty vegetable dish that complements a hearty Roast Leg of Lamb with Herbes de Provence and Potatoes (page 167), rounding it out easily into a meal.

Regional origins are another good guide to pairing dishes. The Chickpea Flour Crêpes Drizzled with Olive Oil (page 211), a dish from Nice that reveals a North African influence, would be appropriate served with other Provençal favorites like vibrant and colorful Ratatouille (page 179) and creamy Salt Cod Brandade (page 73). Aligot (page 204), a rich dish of mashed potatoes, cream, and cheese favored in the Auvergne and other parts of the Massif Central, could hold its own alongside the Beef Brisket with Sauce Gribiche (page 158), from the nearby Rhône Alpes.

Heavier vegetable dishes can also be thought of as the centerpiece of the meal. The hearty Tomato and Eggplant Tian (page 197) or Gratin Dauphinois (page 207) are baked in shallow baking dishes and share many qualities similar to the casserole.

Ratatouille

As soon as tomatoes, zucchini, eggplants, and peppers are ripe in summer, ratatouille is served in homes and restaurants throughout Provence. Some versions call for cooking each vegetable separately, then combining them to finish cooking. However, to save time, home cooks have adapted the dish by cooking all of the vegetables together, as in this recipe.

Bring a saucepan of water to a boil over medium-high heat. Cut an X into the blossom end of each tomato. Using a slotted spoon, carefully lower the tomatoes into the boiling water and cook for 30 seconds. Drain. When the tomatoes are cool enough to handle, slip off the skins and discard. Cut each tomato in half and, using a spoon, dislodge the seeds. Coarsely chop the tomatoes.

In a large, heavy saucepan over medium heat, warm the olive oil. Reduce the heat to medium-low, add the onions, and sauté until translucent, about 2 minutes. Add the eggplant cubes and garlic and cook, stirring frequently, until the eggplants are slightly softened, 3–4 minutes. Add the zucchini and bell peppers and sauté, stirring and turning, until softened, 4–5 minutes longer. Add the chopped tomatoes, thyme, rosemary, bay leaf, salt, and pepper and cook, stirring and turning, for 2–3 minutes longer.

Cover, reduce the heat to low, and cook, stirring occasionally, until the vegetables are soft and have somewhat blended together, about 40 minutes. Stir in the basil and remove from the heat.

Transfer the ratatouille to individual bowls. Serve hot or at room temperature.

8–10 large, ripe, juicy tomatoes, 6–7$\frac{1}{2}$ lb (3–3.75 kg) total weight

2 generous teaspoons extra-virgin olive oil

2 small yellow or white onions, chopped

2 eggplants (aubergines), cut into 1-inch (2.5-cm) cubes

4 cloves garlic, minced

2 zucchini (courgettes), cut into 1-inch (2.5-cm) cubes

2 large red, green, or yellow bell peppers (capsicums), seeded and cut into 1-inch (2.5-cm) pieces

3 sprigs fresh thyme

1 sprig fresh rosemary

1 bay leaf

$\frac{1}{2}$ teaspoon salt

$\frac{1}{2}$ teaspoon freshly ground pepper

$\frac{1}{4}$ cup ($\frac{1}{3}$ oz/10 g) minced fresh basil

MAKES 10 SERVINGS

Sautéed Haricots Verts

2 teaspoons salt, plus extra for garnishing

1½ lb (750 g) young, slender green beans, stem ends trimmed

1 tablespoon unsalted butter

Classic Vinaigrette (page 273)

MAKES 6 SERVINGS

Bring a saucepan of salted water to a boil over medium-high heat. Add the beans and cook until barely tender when pierced with a fork, about 5 minutes. Drain and rinse under running cold water until cool. Drain again and set aside.

In a frying pan or sauté pan over medium heat, melt the butter until it foams. Add the cooled beans and the salt and cook, gently turning the beans, until just heated through, about 2 minutes.

Transfer to a large platter, drizzle with salt and serve at once. Or, omit the butter, reheat the beans, and serve at room temperature with Classic Vinaigrette.

Haricots verts fines, very slender, young green beans, are preferred in France, and many seed varieties have been developed. The ideal size is 5–6 inches (13–15 cm) long and no more than ¼ inch (6 mm) in diameter. The beans are picked before any sign of seed development, so inside they are all flesh. Firm and full of flavor, they require very little cooking.

Braised Fennel with Raisins and Saffron

France shares a border with Spain, one of the world's primary producers of high-quality saffron, so it is not surprising that threads of the vibrant spice, actually the stamens of a particular variety of crocus, appear in some French dishes. Here, the saffron bathes the fennel in a rich golden hue.

Working with one fennel bulb at a time, cut off the stalks and feathery leaves; discard or reserve for another use. Peel away the tough outer layers of the bulbs, then quarter lengthwise.

Place the saffron in a heatproof bowl and cover with the hot broth.

In a frying pan over medium-high heat, warm the olive oil. Add the garlic and the fennel, one cut side down, and sprinkle with the salt and pepper. Reduce the heat to medium and cook, turning occasionally, until the fennel is lightly browned, about 10 minutes. Gradually pour in the saffron-broth mixture and deglaze the pan, scraping the bottom with a wooden spoon to dislodge any browned bits. Raise the heat to high and bring to a boil. Reduce the heat to low, add the raisins, cover, and simmer until the fennel is easily pierced with a fork, 30–40 minutes.

Transfer to a platter and serve hot or at room temperature.

4 medium or 6 small fennel bulbs, 3–4 lb (1.5–2 kg) total weight

¼ teaspoon saffron threads

½ cup (4 fl oz/125 ml) hot chicken broth or water

2 tablespoons extra-virgin olive oil

1 clove garlic, minced

½ teaspoon kosher or sea salt

½ teaspoon freshly ground pepper

¼ cup (1½ oz/45 g) black raisins or golden raisins (sultanas)

MAKES 6 SERVINGS

Roasted Butternut Squash

In France, tough-skinned winter squashes such as butternut are prepared like mashed potatoes. As in this simple preparation, they are simply roasted, then combined with cream and seasonings for a hearty accompaniment to Butter-Roasted Chicken (page 140) or Slow-Braised Pork with Wild Mushrooms (page 161).

Preheat the oven to 350°F (180°C).

Place the squash in a baking dish just large enough to hold it or on a baking sheet. Rub with the olive oil. Bake until the squash is very tender when pierced with a fork, about 1 hour. Remove from the oven.

When the squash is cool enough to handle, cut it in half lengthwise. Remove the seeds and fibers, and discard. Scoop out the flesh and place in a large bowl. Using a fork or potato masher, mash the flesh. Stir in the cream until blended. Season to taste with salt and pepper.

Spoon the squash into a serving bowl and serve at once.

1 butternut squash, about 2 lb (1 kg)

2 teaspoons extra-virgin olive oil

2 tablespoons heavy (double) cream

Salt and freshly ground pepper

MAKES 4 SERVINGS

CORSICA

Roasted Chestnuts

2 lb (1 kg) fresh chestnuts

Dry red or white wine or brandy (optional)

MAKES 6 SERVINGS

Preheat the oven to 500°F (260°C).

Using a sharp knife, cut a shallow X in the flat side of each chestnut. Be careful not to cut through the nutmeat. Arrange the chestnuts in a single layer on a baking sheet and drizzle with the wine, if using.

Roast the chestnuts until the hard skin around each incision peels back and the skin has darkened, 15–20 minutes. Transfer the roasted nuts to a serving bowl, and let cool slightly. Serve warm, letting each guest peel off the skins.

On the streets of French cities from Paris to Bordeaux in winter, the scent of roasting chestnuts fills the air, and vendors scoop the hot nuts into twisted newspaper cones to sell to passers-by. It's also possible to roast chestnuts at home in the oven. They can be eaten out of hand, puréed with cream and sugar for a sweet filling, or used as a savory addition to meat and vegetable dishes.

Chard Gratin

A gratin refers to a dish that has a crunchy crust, which is usually accomplished with cheese, bread crumbs, or a combination. It is a favored French way of cooking and serving vegetables. The vegetables can be first coated with a cream sauce, as here, or with just the topping for a lighter variation.

Preheat the oven to 400°F (200°C). Coat a baking dish with 1 tablespoon of the butter. Place the chard leaves in a large pot, bending them to fit. Add about 5 inches (13 cm) of water and bring to a boil over high heat. Reduce the heat, add the rosemary, cover, and simmer until the leaves are tender, about 15 minutes. Remove the rosemary sprigs. Drain and rinse the chard. Coarsely chop the chard and, using your hands, gently squeeze to remove as much liquid as possible.

In a saucepan over medium-high heat, melt 3 tablespoons of the butter. Remove from the heat and whisk in the flour, salt, and nutmeg. Place over medium-low heat, slowly whisk in the milk, and simmer, stirring, until the sauce thickens, about 15 minutes. Stir in all but 1 tablespoon of the Gruyère and cook until the cheese is melted, about 2 minutes. Spread the chard in the prepared dish. Pour the sauce over the chard, stirring the chard to coat it with the sauce. Sprinkle with the remaining cheese. Dot with the remaining 1/2 tablespoon butter. Bake until the top is browned, about 15 minutes. Serve at once.

4$\frac{1}{2}$ tablespoons (2$\frac{1}{4}$ oz/ 75 g) unsalted butter

3 bunches chard, trimmed

2 sprigs fresh rosemary

3 tablespoons all-purpose (plain) flour

1$\frac{1}{2}$ teaspoons salt

$\frac{1}{4}$ teaspoon grated nutmeg

3 cups (24 fl oz/750 ml) whole milk

$\frac{3}{4}$ cup (3 oz/90 g) shredded Gruyère cheese

MAKES 6 SERVINGS

Zucchini Fritters

**4 zucchini (courgettes), about
1 lb (500 g) total weight**

¼ yellow onion

**¼ cup (1½ oz/45 g)
all-purpose (plain) flour**

½ teaspoon baking powder

Salt

**¼ teaspoon freshly ground
pepper**

1 large egg

Extra-virgin olive oil for frying

MAKES 4 SERVINGS

Trim the stem ends from the zucchini and grate the zucchini on the large holes of a box grater-shredder. Peel the onion and then grate in the same way. Using your hands, gently squeeze the zucchini and onion to remove as much liquid as possible.

In a bowl, stir together the grated zucchini and onion, the flour, baking powder, ½ teaspoon salt, and the pepper. Add the egg and mix well.

Preheat the oven to 200°F (95°C).

Line a platter with paper towels. In a frying pan over medium-high heat, warm 1 tablespoon olive oil. Working in batches, drop the zucchini mixture by heaping teaspoons into the oil, spacing them about 1 inch (2.5 cm) apart. Using the back of a wooden spoon, press down gently on the fritters and fry, turning once, until golden brown on both sides, about 3 minutes total. Using a slotted spatula, transfer to the paper towels to drain. Arrange the fritters on an ovenproof platter and keep warm in the oven while you fry the remaining fritters. Repeat with the remaining zucchini mixture, adding more oil and reducing the heat if necessary. You should have 12–16 fritters.

Sprinkle the fritters with salt and serve at once.

French cooking boasts many types of fritters, both sweet and savory. In the most basic version, slices or pieces of fruits or vegetables are mixed into a seasoned batter and fried. Savory variations, like these fritters, can be served as an appetizer, a first course, or alongside a main dish.

Steamed Artichokes with Aioli

During artichoke season in Provence, the earthy vegetables are often served with aioli, the region's popular and addictive garlic-flavored mayonnaise. Artichokes grown in Provence are often purple tinged and can be considerably smaller than the huge globe artichokes of Brittany. Beurre Blanc (page 268), Sauce Verte (page 268), and Sauce Béarnaise (page 269) are other great options for dipping.

Working with 1 artichoke at a time, trim the stem even with the base. Snap off the small tough leaves around the base. Cut off the upper third of the artichoke, then cut each artichoke in half lengthwise. Rub the cut surface of the artichoke with the lemon half to prevent it from turning brown.

Select a wide saucepan large enough to hold the artichokes in a single layer. Place a steamer rack in the saucepan and add water to reach the bottom of the rack. Place the artichokes, cut side down, on the rack. Bring the water to a simmer over medium heat. Cover and cook until the base of an artichoke is easily pierced with a fork, about 20 minutes.

Transfer the artichokes to individual plates. Serve warm, at room temperature, or chilled, accompanied by the Aioli.

4 medium artichokes

½ lemon

1 cup (8 fl oz/250 ml) Aioli (page 271)

MAKES 4 SERVINGS

CENTRE

Spring Peas with Romaine and Mint

2 lb (1 kg) English peas in their pods

½ head romaine (cos) lettuce

1 tablespoon unsalted butter

2 tablespoons minced shallots

½ cup (4 fl oz/125 ml) chicken broth

Salt and freshly ground pepper

¼ cup (⅓ oz/10 g) finely chopped fresh mint

MAKES 4 SERVINGS

Shell the peas; you should have about 2 cups (10 oz/315 g). Cut the lettuce crosswise into very thin strips.

In a large saucepan over medium-high heat, melt the butter. Add the shallots and sauté until translucent, about 1 minute. Add the peas, lettuce, and chicken broth; cover and cook until the peas are tender to the bite and the lettuce has wilted, about 5 minutes. Season to taste with salt and pepper. Stir in the mint.

Using a slotted spoon, transfer the peas to a serving bowl and serve at once.

Spring peas in the pod are considered a delicacy and are among the most sought-after *primeurs*, or early spring vegetables. Small, sweet, and tender, they require very little cooking and minimal seasonings. Fresh mint is sometimes added, as here.

Tomato and Eggplant Tian

A *tian* is both a Provençal cooking vessel and a finished dish. The vessel is usually oval, slightly deeper than a gratin dish, and is made of terra-cotta. It is typically used for baking vegetables, but it can be used for meats as well. Try this dish at the peak of summer when the vegetables are at their ripest.

Preheat the oven to 400°F (200°C).

Trim off the stem ends from the eggplants and cut the eggplants crosswise into slices $1/2$ inch (12 mm) thick. Arrange the slices in a single layer on a baking sheet. Brush both sides with $1-1^1/2$ tablespoons of the olive oil and sprinkle with $1/2$ teaspoon of the salt and $1/4$ teaspoon of the pepper.

Cook until the undersides of the eggplant slices are lightly browned and a crust has formed on the tops, about 15 minutes. Turn the slices and cook until the insides are soft and the undersides are browned, about 10 minutes longer.

Meanwhile, coarsely chop the tomatoes and put them in a bowl with their juice. Add the remaining $1/2$ teaspoon salt, the remaining $1/4$ teaspoon pepper, the garlic, and thyme.

Raise the oven temperature to 450°F (230°C). Coat a gratin dish with the remaining $2^1/2$-3 tablespoons olive oil.

Arrange the eggplant slices in a layer in the prepared gratin dish, overlapping them slightly. Sprinkle with half of the basil. Spread the tomato mixture over the eggplant, slightly lifting the slices to let the juices run underneath. Sprinkle evenly with the bread crumbs and dot with the butter.

Bake until the tomatoes are bubbling and the bread crumbs are browned, 20–25 minutes. Sprinkle the *tian* with the remaining basil and serve at once.

2 globe or 4 Asian (slender) eggplants (aubergines)

4 tablespoons (2 fl oz/60 ml) extra-virgin olive oil

1 teaspoon salt

$1/2$ teaspoon freshly ground pepper

6 ripe, juicy tomatoes, about 3 lb (1.5 g) total weight

1 clove garlic, minced

1 teaspoon fresh thyme leaves

$1/4$ cup ($1/3$ oz/10 g) chopped fresh basil

$1/4$ cup (1 oz/30 g) coarse dried bread crumbs

1 tablespoon unsalted butter, cut into small pieces

MAKES 6–8 SERVINGS

Baked Leeks with Bread Crumbs

6 tablespoons (3 oz/90 g) unsalted butter

2 tablespoons minced shallots

6–8 leeks, about 3 lb (500 g) total weight, white and pale green parts, chopped

1 teaspoon salt

3/4 teaspoon freshly ground white pepper

2 cups (16 fl oz/500 ml) whole milk, plus extra as needed

3 tablespoons all-purpose (plain) flour

1/4 teaspoon cayenne pepper

1/2 cup (2 oz/60 g) shredded Gruyère cheese

1/2 cup (1 oz/30 g) fresh bread crumbs

MAKES 6 SERVINGS

Preheat the oven to 400°F (200°C).

In a frying pan over medium-high heat, melt 2 tablespoons of the butter until it foams. Add the shallots, leeks, and 1/2 teaspoon each of the salt and pepper. Reduce the heat to medium and cook, stirring often, until the leeks are translucent and very soft, about 15 minutes. Set aside.

In a small saucepan over medium heat, cook the milk until small bubbles appear around the edge of the pan. Cover and remove from the heat.

In a saucepan over medium-high heat, melt 3 tablespoons of the butter until it foams. Remove from the heat and whisk in the flour, the remaining 1/2 teaspoon salt, the remaining 1/4 teaspoon pepper, and the cayenne to make a roux. Return the pan to medium-low heat, slowly whisk in the hot milk, and simmer, stirring, until the sauce thickens, about 15 minutes. If the sauce is too thin, increase the heat; if it is too thick, whisk in a little more milk. Stir in the leek mixture.

Pour the mixture into a baking or gratin dish. Sprinkle evenly with the cheese and the bread crumbs and dot with the remaining 1 tablespoon butter.

Bake until the cheese and bread crumb topping is golden and the gratin is bubbly, 20–30 minutes. Serve at once.

Leeks are the queens of the onion family and have pride of place in French cuisine, where they appear in vinaigrettes, quiches, stews, and gratins such as this one. Bursting with flavor, this dish works well as a first course, a main course, or a side dish with meat and poultry.

Mushrooms en Papillote

Baking mushrooms in a sealed parchment packet, or *en papillote*, allows them to cook through without browning, as they would if sautéed. Serving them in the package makes an attractive presentation, as well as a flavorful partner to light poultry and fish dishes.

Preheat the oven to 375°F (190°C).

Cut parchment (baking) paper into an 18-by-11-inch (45-by-28-cm) rectangle. Fold the rectangle in half crosswise. Open the parchment and coat with the 1 tablespoon butter. Place the rectangle, buttered side up, on a baking sheet.

Cut the mushrooms into bite-size pieces and place in a bowl. Add the salt, pepper, butter pieces, lemon juice, and parsley and toss well. Spread the mushrooms over one half of the prepared parchment paper. Fold the other half of the parchment rectangle over the mushrooms and fold the vertical edges over twice, working your way along the paper's edge to end with a twist on both ends. Place the package on a rimmed baking sheet.

Bake until the parchment packet is puffed and the mushrooms are cooked through, about 15 minutes. Transfer the parchment packet to a platter, carefully open the packet, and serve at once.

1 tablespoon unsalted butter, plus 1 tablespoon unsalted butter, cut into small pieces

1 lb (500 g) mushrooms such as chanterelle, shiitake, trumpet, portobello, or a mixture, brushed clean

½ teaspoon salt

¼ teaspoon freshly ground pepper

1 teaspoon fresh lemon juice

2 tablespoons chopped fresh flat-leaf (Italian) parsley

MAKES 4–6 SERVINGS

Pommes Anna

5 tablespoons (2¹⁄₂ oz/75 g) unsalted butter

1¹⁄₂ lb (750 g) potatoes

Salt and freshly ground pepper

MAKES 6 SERVINGS

Preheat the oven to 375°F (190°C). Coat a 9-inch (23-cm) pie pan or Pommes Anna pan (page 43) with 1 tablespoon of the butter.

Peel the potatoes, then rinse, and pat dry with paper towels. Using the thin slicing blade on a mandoline, or a very sharp chef's knife, cut the potatoes into slices ¹⁄₈ inch (3 mm) thick.

In a large saucepan over medium heat, melt the remaining 4 tablespoons butter until it foams. Set aside.

Arrange some of the potato slices in a single layer in the prepared pan, overlapping them just slightly. Lightly sprinkle with salt and pepper and drizzle some of the melted butter over the top. Repeat the layering process until all of the potato slices have been used.

Bake in the oven until the potatoes are tender when pierced with a fork and the top is crisp and golden in color, 45–60 minutes. Transfer to a wire rack and let stand for 5 minutes.

Run a table knife around the edge of the pan, then place a serving plate over the top and invert the pan and plate together to unmold. Replace any potatoes that may have stuck to the pan. Cut into wedges and serve at once.

This famous French potato gratin was created in honor of Anna Deslions, a celebrated courtesan of nineteenth century Paris, by the Café des Anglais, where she often dined. The layered potatoes are crisp and golden on the bottom and perfectly tender on top. Pommes Anna makes an impressive presentation when the baking dish is inverted to display the overlapping crispy potatoes.

Gratin Dauphinois

This rich potato dish is a specialty of the Dauphiné area of France, which includes the gastronomic heartland of Lyons. It is enjoyed all over the country for its golden, cheese-topped crust and creamy potatoes beneath. This dish can be served with heartier fare such as roast pork, veal, and chops.

Preheat the oven to 425°F (220°C). Rub a flameproof baking dish with the garlic, then coat it with the 1 tablespoon butter.

Peel the potatoes. Using the thin slicing blade on a mandoline, if possible, cut the potatoes into slices $1/8$ inch (3 mm) thick. Arrange half of the potato slices in a single layer in the prepared baking dish, overlapping them slightly. Sprinkle evenly with $1/2$ teaspoon of the salt, $1/2$ teaspoon of the pepper, 1 teaspoon of the thyme, and half of the cheese. Dot with half of the butter pieces. Add another layer of potato slices and top with the remaining $1/2$ teaspoon salt, the remaining $1/2$ teaspoon pepper, and the remaining 1 teaspoon thyme. Sprinkle evenly with the remaining cheese and butter pieces.

In a small saucepan over medium-high heat, bring the milk to a boil. Remove from the heat and pour over the potato slices. Place the baking dish over medium-low heat and cook until the milk begins to simmer. Immediately transfer to the oven.

Cook until the potatoes are easily pierced with a fork, the milk has been absorbed, and the top is slightly golden, 35–45 minutes.

Transfer the dish to a wire rack and let stand for 5 minutes. Serve at once.

1 clove garlic, crushed

1 tablespoon unsalted butter, plus 2 tablespoons unsalted butter, cut into small pieces

2 lb (1 kg) baking potatoes

1 teaspoon kosher or sea salt

1 teaspoon freshly ground pepper

2 teaspoons minced fresh thyme, or 1 teaspoon dried thyme

$1/4$ lb (125 g) Swiss cheese, shredded

1 cup (8 fl oz/250 ml) whole milk

MAKES 6 SERVINGS

Le Puy Lentils

1¹⁄₂ cups (10¹⁄₂ oz/330 g)
Le Puy lentils

2 bay leaves

1¹⁄₂ teaspoons salt

MAKES 4 SERVINGS

Place the lentils in a colander and pick them over, discarding any misshapen lentils or stones. Rinse under running cold water and drain.

In a saucepan over medium-high heat, combine the lentils, bay leaves, salt, and 5 cups (40 fl oz/1.25 l) water and bring to a boil. Reduce the heat to medium-low and simmer until the lentils are tender, 20–30 minutes. Drain and let cool.

Spoon the lentils into a warmed serving bowl and serve at once.

The Le Puy region in central France is noted for its tiny, green lentils, called *lentils du Puy*. They hold their shape when cooked and have a finer flavor than common brown lentils. Enjoy them as a side dish with Pork Rillettes (page 67) or sausages, or seasoned with olive oil and vinegar to make a salad.

Fava Beans with Garlic and Thyme

2 tablespoons extra-virgin olive oil

2 cloves garlic, minced

2 lb (1 kg) fava (broad) beans, shelled and skinned

2 tablespoons fresh thyme leaves

Salt and freshly ground pepper

MAKES 4 SERVINGS

In a large, heavy saucepan over medium heat, warm the olive oil. Add the garlic and sauté just until the garlic softens, 1–2 minutes. Add the fava beans and sauté until they begin to change color, 4–5 minutes. Add the thyme and ¹⁄₂ cup (4 fl oz/ 125 ml) water, and season to taste with salt and pepper. Reduce the heat to low, cover, and cook until the beans are tender and the water has evaporated, 5–6 minutes.

Transfer the beans to a warmed serving dish and serve at once.

Fava beans crop up in spring gardens throughout France. Look for soft green pods packed with pale green beans that resemble lima beans.

Chickpea Flour Crêpes Drizzled with Olive Oil

A visit to Nice on the French Riviera isn't complete without stopping for *socca*, the hot chickpea flour crêpes that vendors sell in and around the marketplace. The slightly thick pancakes are torn into pieces, sprinkled with coarse sea salt, and eaten out of hand, preferably accompanied by a glass of local red wine. Serve them drizzled with olive oil.

In a bowl, whisk together the flour, salt, 1 tablespoon of the olive oil, and ¹/₂ cup (4 fl oz/125 ml) water. Add a little more water as needed to achieve a thick, smooth batter that is thicker than classic pancake batter.

In an 8- or 9-inch (20- or 23-cm) nonstick frying pan over medium-high heat, warm 1¹/₂ teaspoons of the olive oil. Ladle ¹/₄–¹/₃ cup (2–3 fl oz/60–80 ml) of the batter into the pan, tilting and swirling the pan to coat the bottom with the batter. Cook until the edges are firm and separate slightly from the pan, about 2 minutes. Using a spatula, turn the crêpe and cook until the bottom has golden brown spots, 1–2 minutes longer. Transfer the crêpe to a warmed platter. Repeat with the remaining olive oil and batter to make 2 more crêpes.

Cut the crêpes into wedges. Sprinkle with coarse sea salt and drizzle with olive oil. Serve at once while still warm.

1 cup (4 oz/125 g) plus 1 tablespoon chickpea (garbanzo bean) flour

1 teaspoon kosher or sea salt

2¹/₂ tablespoons extra-virgin olive oil, plus extra for drizzling

Coarse sea salt for serving

MAKES 6 SERVINGS

Les Desserts and Pâtisseries

About Les Desserts and Pâtisseries

French cuisine offers much to enjoy, but few would dispute that desserts and pastries are its crowning achievements. French desserts and pastries are memorable for their intense flavors, often focused on a single ingredient: caramel or cream, chocolate or fruit.

Following as they do on the heels of a cheese course and, in the case of formal dinners, a separate fruit course, French desserts emphasize quality over quantity. As is the case with the hors d'oeuvre, some are meant just as an exquisite sweet mouthful to close the meal.

THE CHEESE COURSE

A selection of cheeses, offered after the main course and before or in place of dessert, is not really considered an extra flourish at the French table, but rather an integral part of the meal. To make a cheese plate, visit a good cheese shop and ask to sample a variety of French cheeses. Choose at least three types with either contrasting or complementary qualities. You might present a "flight" of one type of cheese, aged to different degrees; an assortment of cheeses made from different kinds of milk, (cow's, goat's, and sheep's); or an assortment of cheeses from different families, offering different pungencies and textures (keeping in mind that French cheese usually tastes less pungent than it might smell, and tends to be on the soft side, usually softer than Cheddar). For a platter with more than three cheeses, add a blue for variety. If you happen to come upon one outstanding cheese, you can serve it alone in a dramatic starring role.

Many cheese shops will also offer many good accompaniments to cheeses, such as baguettes, crackers, nuts, and fruit pastes. Fresh fruit is usually a great partner for cheese, as is honey. Ask the cheese monger for tips on pairing wines with your particular cheeses: some match nicely with a sweet dessert wine, while a fresh goat cheese is great with a crisp white, and more pungent washed-rind cheeses and blues work well with red wine or even port. Serving a wine from the same region as the cheese is always a good bet. For more details on creating a cheese plate, see page 216.

FRUIT DESSERTS

Fruit tarts are a French specialty, and you can find delicious choices for every time of year. *Fraises des bois*, or wild strawberries, are a cherished treat and grace tarts both large and small in the late spring when they appear (Fraises des Bois Tartlets, page 225). When autumn arrives with a chill in the air, serve rich Tarte Tatin (page 222), an upside-down tart showcasing tender apples glistening with caramel. A simple tart shell filled with citrus curd is a perfectly elegant way to enjoy winter fruit (Tarte au Citron, page 226).

Beloved fruits find their way into other types of desserts as well. Perfectly ripe melons, an obsession in the South of France especially, are often enjoyed on their own as dessert. From the cherry groves of rural central France comes clafouti, a custardy cake dotted with cherries (page 233). Poached fruits, especially pears (page 230), are a favorite homemade dessert in France. The famous prunes of Agen, in southwest France, are steeped in Armagnac and appear in both sweet and savory dishes, sometimes partnering with freshly whipped Crème Chantilly (page 271).

OTHER SWEETS

Chocolate, which was at first met with suspicion when it arrived in France in the seventeenth century, now finds its greatest expression in French confections and desserts. But chocolate also takes well to simple preparations, and nothing offers more pleasure than a Flourless Chocolate Cake (page 257) or Chocolate Pots de Crème (page 261), which are surprisingly easy to make at home.

Custards and creams are another essential part of the dessert menu, and two choices that are especially dear to the French are *îles flottantes* and *coeur à la crème*. The first, whose name means "floating islands" (page 250), looks dramatic—two egg-shaped mounds of frothy meringue floating in a sea of vanilla custard. Coeur à la Crème (page 221), similarly, makes a grand entrance when the creamy white "heart of cream," made of cream cheese and crème fraîche, is freed from its mold and surrounded with bright jewel-toned berry coulis, but to the French this is nostalgic comfort food at its best.

Pastries, whether they are Butter Croissants for breakfast (page 264) or Éclairs dipped in velvety chocolate ganache (page 263) for dessert, are forever embedded into the French culture and are on the menu or table just about anywhere you go.

COFFEE AND DIGESTIFS

In France coffee always appears after dessert, and takes the form of a single shot of espresso, which is believed to stimulate digestion. It may be followed by a *digestif*, the bookend to the *apéritif*. Brandy and marc are stiffer possibilities, while herbal liqueurs such as Chartreuse and Bénédictine have a long history and are enjoying a resurgence in popularity.

Le Fromage

France produces hundreds of different cow's, sheep's, and goat's milk cheeses, or *fromages*, ranging from fresh and mild to aged and pungent. No truly French meal is complete without a cheese course, served at the end of the savory part of the meal and before the sweets.

THE CHEESE PLATE

After the main course, a single cheese might be offered. Or, a dozen or more might be presented from which the diners choose up to four or five varieties. Such an array of cheeses is best tasted beginning with mild flavors and working up to strong ones. The selection of cheeses may be composed of all goat cheeses, all cheeses from one region, a variety of blue cheeses, or three or four cheeses of different types and consistencies, such as a triple-cream cow's milk cheese, an herb-coated sheep's milk cheese, and a blue-veined cheese.

It is best to arrange cheeses on a flat surface, such as a wooden cutting board or marble slab, which will make them easier to cut. Cheeses should also not be placed too close together so their flavors stay separate.

BUYING AND STORING CHEESE

To keep cheese fresh, purchase just enough for your particular occasion and more only if you serve it often. Quality cheese should be wrapped in butcher paper, which is best, or plastic. It should remain this way until you are ready to eat it as this prevents the cheese from drying out; it also keeps the cheese from absorbing odors from other foods.

Ideally, cheeses should be stored in the refrigerator or a cool, dark room until about 30 minutes before serving. In order to get the best flavor and all of the characteristics that the cheese has to offer, it should be eaten at room temperature.

FRENCH CHEESE

Camembert Soft, ripened unpasteurized cow's milk cheese with an edible powdery white rind; similar to Brie.

Morbier Mild, smooth-textured cow's milk cheese. Notable for the blue-black streak of ash running through its middle.

Brin d'Amour Soft white sheep's milk cheese from Corsica that is coated with juniper berries, pepper, rosemary, and winter savory.

Mimolette Nutty aged cow's milk cheese from Lille with an orange interior.

Cantal Hard AOC cheese made from cow's milk, with a sweet buttery flavor that gets earthier and tangier as it ages.

Bleu d'Auvergne Cow's milk blue cheese and cousin of Roquefort.

Vacherin Mont d'Or Soft, pungent AOC cow's milk cheese with a white rind and a creamy ivory interior.

Crottin de Chavignol Round cheese made from goat's milk and enjoyed young, creamy, and white, or aged and nutty, with a thick gray rind.

Saint-Nectaire Soft, pressed AOC cow's milk cheese with a grayish rind and a nutty flavor.

Brie The "king of cheese," this creamy unpasteurized cow's milk cheese is one of the oldest of all French cheeses.

Le Chocolat

Some of the world's finest chocolates are made in France, and many artisanal chocolate makers have set up shops, or *chocolateries,* throughout the country. This one ingredient offers endless options to end a meal, from decadent desserts to the most elegant bonbons, truffles, or pralines.

Chocolate is produced from cacao beans that grow in pods and sprout from the trunk and large branches of the cacao tree *(Theobroma cacao),* which thrives in the tropical climates of West Africa and Central and South America. Once the beans are imported, the process of extracting the chocolate is quite painstaking and involves several steps such as fermentation, drying, and roasting. After the beans have

been roasted, the shell is easy to crack, and the cacao "nibs" within are removed. The nibs are ground to produce chocolate liquor, a dark brown paste consisting of cocoa butter, or cocoa fat, and cocoa mass. The paste cools and hardens into unsweetened chocolate.

Chocolate first arrived in France in the seventeenth century when Jewish confectioners set up processing operations in Bayonne, in

Southwestern France, after fleeing the inquisition on the Iberian Peninsula. Chocolate was not well received at first, but its popularity grew in 1615 when Louis XIII took a Spanish bride who served it to the French court.

Today, France is a leading producer of chocolate and boasts many high-end brands, the most famous being Valrhona, and the French have also become renowned for their chocolate confections. Chocolate shops, especially those in Paris, are filled with such elaborate displays of chocolate artistry that they resemble jewelry stores.

Within each region, chocolate is given flavors specific to that area. For example, in

Provence, chocolate is infused with lavender, and in the north near the Spanish border, chocolate is spiced with chile flakes. In the many famed chocolate shops of Paris, *chocolatiers* experiment by adding exotic spices, fruits, and tea in their chocolate.

CHOOSING CHOCOLATE

When selecting chocolate, choose a high-quality brand of whatever type is called for in the recipe; if serving chocolate alone, buy from a reputable source.

Several types of chocolate are available. Unsweetened chocolate is pure chocolate liquor and is used as the base for all other types of chocolate, except for white.

Bittersweet, a common European term, and semisweet, a common American term and also known as plain, are produced when sugar is added to chocolate liquor. Many companies list the cocoa butter content of their dark chocolate on the packaging. This content can be used to judge whether a particular brand of chocolate is suitable for the dessert you are making. For example, if a chocolate contains 40 percent cocoa butter, it could be used for a recipe that calls for semisweet chocolate. When a less sweet chocolate is desired, look for one with a higher content, such as 70 percent.

White chocolate is made from cocoa butter, sugar, and milk solids, and does not contain chocolate liquor or cocoa solids.

FROM THE CHOCOLATERIE

Below are some common types of chocolate that can be found at a *chocolaterie*.

Poudre de cacoa, "cocoa powder," is used to make hot chocolate or to dust truffles. Dense and rich, it is made by finely grinding the compressed nibs of cacao beans after most of the cocoa butter has been removed. It comes

in two forms: sweetened and unsweetened. Most French cafés use the sweetened powder to make *chocolat chaud* or hot chocolate, while the unsweetened powder is used for coating truffles and decorating cakes.

Chocolat noir aux noisettes is literally "dark chocolate with nuts." The French are firm believers in eating a small amount of dark chocolate–*chocolat noir*–for good health. The addition of roasted nuts is popular, and the most favored chocolate-nut pairing is with hazelnuts (filberts), or *noisettes*.

Chocolat au lait translates as "milk chocolate." Most mass-produced milk chocolate is cloyingly sweet, but a well-crafted bar is creamy, rich, and delicate. The amount of cacao varies, but it is usually no more than 45 percent. Although milk chocolate is often filled with caramel and nuts, plain bars are a classic snack for French children who like to eat them in a fresh baguette.

Truffes au chocolat, "chocolate truffles," are named after the famous fungi to which they resemble. In taste, however, they are balls of creamy chocolate rolled in cocoa powder. The traditional recipe is very easy to make: ganache, a mix of dark chocolate and cream, is formed into a ball, dipped in a thin coating of chocolate, and then rolled in cocoa.

Bonbons de chocolat are elegant bonbons. These little gems of chocolate are usually filled with chocolate ganache that is flavored with anything from candied citrus peel or coconut to such unusual recent additions as green tea or black pepper. The classic bonbon is square, usually with fine parallel lines or a dusting of cocoa on top. Hand-dipped versions are especially favored, as their thin coating does not detract from the ganache inside. Sold in tall, rectangular boxes called *ballotins*, French bonbons are pricey but well worth it, and are always a popular gift.

Coeur à la Crème

This festive dessert is a favorite with children because of its mild, sweet flavor and creamy consistency. Adults also like the sweetened cream cheese spooned into heart-shaped molds and served with fresh fruit such as raspberries.

Line 4 heart-shaped *coeur à la crème* molds with damp cheesecloth (muslin); the edges should hang over the rims of the molds. Set the molds on a baking sheet.

In a bowl, using an electric mixer, beat together the cream cheese and the confectioners' sugar to taste. Whisk in the Crème Fraîche, vanilla, and lemon juice. Divide the cream cheese mixture among the prepared molds and fold the overhanging cheesecloth over the top. Refrigerate the molds on the baking sheet overnight to drain any excess liquid.

Gently turn the cheese out into your hand and unwrap the cheesecloth. Place each heart on a dessert plate and let stand for 10–15 minutes.

Serve with berries and Raspberry Coulis, if using, and mint sprigs.

½ lb (250 g) cream cheese, at room temperature

¼–½ cup (1–2 oz/30–60 g) confectioners' (icing) sugar

⅓ cup (3 fl oz/80 ml) Crème Fraîche (page 275 or purchased)

¼ teaspoon pure vanilla extract

¼ teaspoon fresh lemon juice

Raspberries, blueberries, or other fruits for serving (optional)

Raspberry Coulis (page 271) for serving (optional)

Mint sprigs for garnish (optional)

MAKES 4 SERVINGS

Tarte Tatin

All-purpose (plain) flour for dusting

1 sheet puff pastry, thawed if frozen

½ cup (¼ lb/500 g) unsalted butter

½ cup (4 oz/125 g) sugar

10–11 sweet apples, such as Gala or Golden Delicious, peeled, halved, and cored

MAKES 6–8 SERVINGS

On a lightly floured work surface, roll out the pastry until it is ¼ inch (6 mm) thick. Invert a 9-inch (23-cm) cast-iron frying pan or flameproof baking dish on top of the pastry. Using a knife, cut a circle of dough the same size as the top of the pan. Place the pastry round on a piece of aluminum foil, cover with another piece of foil, and refrigerate until ready to use.

Preheat the oven to 375°F (165°C). Heavily coat the sides and bottom of the pan with the butter and sprinkle with the sugar.

Arrange the apple halves, slightly tilted, in a concentric circle in the pan, packing them in as tightly as you can. Place 4 or 5 halves in the center. Place the pan over medium heat and cook until the pan juices color and bubble and the apples begin to soften, 20–25 minutes.

Transfer the pan to the oven and bake until the apples darken in color and are soft when pierced with a fork, 20–25 minutes. Remove from the oven and cover with the chilled pastry round. Return to the oven and bake until the pastry is puffed and golden, about 25 minutes longer.

Remove from the oven. Run a knife along the edge of the pan to loosen the tart. Place a large plate over the top of the pan and, using potholders, invert them together to unmold the tart. Replace any apple pieces that have stuck to the pan.

Serve the tart hot, warm, or at room temperature.

Although this upside-down apple tart originated in the Loire region south of Paris, it now belongs to the entire French culinary lexicon. The invention of the dessert is attributed to the Tatin sisters, who started making it at their hotel-restaurant in the late twentieth century. Today, one can find *tarte tatin* made with different fruits and even savory versions, but the original was prepared only with apples.

Fraises des Bois Tartlets

Fraises des bois, the most exquisite of all strawberry varieties, have an intensely sweet, deep strawberry flavor. Most are cultivated now, but the original strains were wild, hence the name "forest strawberries." They are perfect to use in tartlets because of their tiny size and the powerful flavor each small berry delivers. If you can't find *fraises des bois*, use another variety of strawberry.

Preheat the oven to 425°F (220°C). Have ready four 4-inch (10-cm) tartlet pans with removable bottoms. Divide the dough into 4 pieces. Working with 1 piece at a time and keeping the others refrigerated, on a floured work surface, roll out the first piece of dough ¼ inch (6 mm) thick. Using a knife, cut out a round of dough ½ inch (12 mm) larger than the size of a tartlet pan; discard the scraps or reserve for another use. Slip a knife or icing spatula under the cutout and gently press into a tartlet pan, trimming the edges as needed. Repeat with the remaining 3 pieces of dough. Cut a circle of parchment paper for each pan. Line the crust with the parchment circles and fill with pie weights or dried beans.

Bake for 10 minutes. Remove from the oven and lift out the weights and parchment paper. Prick any bubbles with the tines of a fork and return to the oven until golden, 4–5 minutes longer. Transfer to a wire rack and let cool completely.

In small saucepan over low heat, warm the jelly, stirring, until melted. Remove from the heat. Spoon just enough of the jelly into each cooled pastry shell to thinly coat the bottom, tilting the pan from side to side to coat evenly. Gently reheat the jelly, if necessary, to thin it. Spoon the Crème Pâtissière into each shell to make a layer ¼–⅓ inch (6–9 mm) thick. Top with the strawberries. Spoon jelly over the berries to coat them. Cover and refrigerate for at least 1 hour or up to 12 hours.

Unmold the tartlets and place on dessert plates. Let stand at room temperature for 15–20 minutes before serving.

Tart Dough (page 274)

½ cup (5 oz/155 g) strawberry jelly

Crème Pâtissière (page 275)

3 cups (12 oz/375 g) *fraises des bois* **or sliced strawberries**

MAKES 4 SERVINGS

Tarte au Citron

For the pastry

1¹⁄₂ cups (7¹⁄₂ oz/235 g) all-purpose (plain) flour

¹⁄₂ cup (4 oz/125 g) unsalted butter, at room temperature

¹⁄₄ cup (2 oz/60 g) granulated sugar

1 large egg

For the filling

3–4 lemons

³⁄₄ cup (6 oz/185 g) granulated sugar

1 large egg, plus 1 large egg yolk

3 tablespoons unsalted butter, melted

Confectioners' (icing) sugar for dusting

MAKES 6 SERVINGS

Preheat the oven to 350°F (180°C). Have ready a 9-inch (23-cm) tart pan with a removable bottom.

To make the pastry, in a bowl, combine the flour and sugar and stir until well blended. Add the butter and, using your fingertips, rub it together until the mixture is crumbly. Add the egg and, using a fork, mix it into the dough. Using your fingers, press the dough evenly into the bottom and up the sides of the tart pan; the crust should be about ¹⁄₄ inch (6 mm) thick.

Line the crust with aluminum foil or parchment (baking) paper and fill with pie weights or dried beans. Bake until slightly firm, about 10 minutes. Remove from the oven and lift out the weights and foil. Prick any bubbles with a fork. Return to the oven and bake until the crust is firm and barely colored, about 5 minutes longer. Transfer to a wire rack.

To make the filling, finely grate the zest of 2 of the lemons. Halve and juice as many lemons as needed to yield ³⁄₄ cup (6 fl oz/180 ml) juice.

In a bowl, using an electric mixer, beat the granulated sugar, egg, and egg yolk until pale yellow. Gradually pour in the melted butter, beating constantly. Stir in the lemon zest and juice. Gently spoon the filling into the cooled pastry shell. Bake until the crust is golden and the filling is lightly golden and firm to the touch, about 25 minutes. Transfer to a wire rack to cool completely.

Dust the tart with confectioners' sugar, cut into wedges, and serve at once.

France has a small citrus-growing region near Menton on the Riviera bordering Italy that is famous for its lemons and oranges. In winter, the scent of citrus fills the markets of the town, and the bakery windows are lined with lemon tarts or *tartes au citron*. There are many versions of the tart, some with more or less butter or eggs. This recipe is on the buttery side.

Apple Beignets

Normandy is one of France's major apple-producing areas, and the culinary tradition of the region includes countless ways to use apples and their products. Apple fritters, or beignets, are one of them. The apples might be coarsely chopped and mixed into the batter as done here, or cut into slices and dipped in the batter before frying.

In a bowl, stir together the flour, cornstarch, salt, and baking powder. Beat in the milk just until a batter forms.

Pour the oil to a depth of 2 inches (5 cm) in a deep fryer or deep, heavy frying pan and heat to 350°F (180°C) on a deep-frying thermometer.

Line a plate with paper towels. Stir the apples into the batter. Working in batches, drop the batter by heaping tablespoonfuls into the oil; do not crowd the pan. Fry, turning once, until the beignets are just golden on all sides, 3–4 minutes total. Using a slotted spoon, transfer to the paper towels to drain.

Sprinkle the beignets with the confectioners' sugar and serve at once.

1³/₄ cups (9 oz/280 g) all-purpose (plain) flour

¹/₄ cup (1 oz/30 g) cornstarch (cornflour)

¹/₂ teaspoon salt

1 tablespoon baking powder

2 cups (16 fl oz/500 ml) whole milk

Grapeseed, canola, or other light vegetable oil for deep-frying

3 cups (12 oz/375 g) peeled, cored, and coarsely chopped apples

Confectioners' (icing) sugar for dusting

MAKES 8 SERVINGS

Poached Pears with Crème Fraîche Ice Cream

For the ice cream

1 cup (8 fl oz/250 ml) half-and-half (half cream)

1 cup (8 fl oz/250 ml) heavy (double) cream

¾ cup (6 oz/185 g) sugar

Pinch of salt

½ vanilla bean pod, split

5 large egg yolks

1 cup (8 fl oz/250 ml) Crème Fraîche (page 275 or purchased)

4 Bosc pears

1 bottle (24 fl oz/750 ml) red wine such as Pinot Noir or Merlot

3 tablespoons sugar

½ cup (4 fl oz/125 ml) heavy (double) cream

1 teaspoon finely chopped fresh rosemary

MAKES 4 SERVINGS

To make the ice cream, in a large heavy saucepan over medium heat, combine the half-and-half, cream, sugar, and salt. Scrape the seeds from the vanilla pod into the pan and add the pod. Cook, stirring, until the sugar dissolves, about 5 minutes.

In a bowl, whisk the egg yolks until pale yellow, about 2 minutes. Gradually whisk the yolks into the hot cream mixture and cook, stirring constantly, until the mixture thickens enough to coat the back of a metal spoon, and a finger scraped across it leaves a path, about 6 minutes. Remove from the heat and whisk in the Crème Fraîche. Let cool to room temperature, then refrigerate until cold, about 2 hours. Pour into an ice-cream maker and freeze according to the manufacturer's instructions. Transfer the ice cream to a freezer-safe container, cover, and freeze until firm, at least 8 hours or up to 24 hours.

When the ice cream is ready, peel and halve the pears lengthwise, leaving the stem intact on one of the halves. Scoop out and discard the seeds and core. Remove the string that runs down the center from the stem to the cavity.

In a frying pan large enough to hold all the pear halves in a single layer, combine the wine and 2 tablespoons of the sugar and bring to a boil over medium heat, stirring to dissolve the sugar. Raise the heat to high and cook until a light syrup has formed, 3–4 minutes. Reduce the heat to low, add the pears, and poach until just tender, 20–30 minutes; do not overcook the pears or they will become mushy.

Transfer the pears with the poaching liquid to a nonreactive bowl and let stand for several hours at room temperature, turning the pears occasionally. They will become a deep garnet color as they absorb the wine.

In a small bowl, mix together the cream, the remaining 1 tablespoon sugar, and the chopped rosemary.

Place 2 pear halves on each dessert plate. Spoon a few spoonfuls of the cream mixture and some of the poaching liquid onto the pear on each plate. Add a scoop of the ice cream and serve at once.

Poached in a regional red wine and served with a scoop of subtle crème fraîche ice cream, fruits such as pears, apples, and quinces make a glamorous end to a meal. The fruits turn a striking deep red as they absorb the poaching liquid, so be sure to turn them often so they color evenly.

Cherry Clafouti

Cherry clafouti originally hails from the Limousin region in central France, an area well known for its cherries, but it is now found on menus throughout France. Purists claim that the cherries must be left unpitted. If you choose this style, be sure to warn your guests.

Preheat the oven to 350°F (180°C). Coat a 9- or 10-inch (23- or 25-cm) round baking dish with the butter.

In a bowl, using an electric mixer on medium speed, beat the milk, cream, flour, eggs, granulated sugar, vanilla, and salt until frothy, about 5 minutes.

Pour enough of the batter into the prepared baking dish to cover the bottom with a layer about 1/4 inch (6 mm) deep. Bake for 2 minutes, then carefully remove the pan from the oven.

Scatter the cherries in a single layer over the batter. Pour the remaining batter over the cherries. Return to the oven and bake until puffed and browned and a knife inserted into the center comes out clean, 30–35 minutes.

Dust the clafouti with confectioners' sugar and serve at once.

1 teaspoon unsalted butter

1 cup (8 fl oz/250 ml) whole milk

1/4 cup (2 fl oz/60 ml) heavy (double) cream

2/3 cup (3 1/2 oz/105 g) all-purpose (plain) flour

3 large eggs

1/3 cup (3 oz/90 g) granulated sugar

1 teaspoon pure vanilla extract

1/4 teaspoon salt

4 cups (2 1/2 lb/1.25 g) stemmed fresh cherries, pitted

Confectioners' (icing) sugar for dusting

MAKES 6–8 SERVINGS

Crêpes Suzette

For the batter

**⅓ cup (2½ oz/60 g)
all-purpose (plain) flour**

1 teaspoon sugar

½ teaspoon salt

4 large eggs

**1¾ cups (14 fl oz/430 ml)
whole milk, plus extra as
needed**

3 tablespoons unsalted butter

Suzette Butter (page 275)

**6 tablespoons (3 fl oz/90 ml)
brandy**

3 tablespoons Grand Marnier

**Thin strips of orange zest
for garnish**

MAKES 6 SERVINGS

To make the batter, in a small bowl, whisk together the flour, sugar, and salt. In a bowl, whisk together the eggs and the 1¾ cups milk. Gradually whisk in the flour mixture to make a thin, lump-free batter. Cover and refrigerate for 2 hours.

When ready to cook, stir the batter; it should be the consistency of heavy cream. If it is too thick, thin with a little more milk. Heat a 12-inch (30-cm) crêpe pan or frying pan, preferably nonstick, over medium heat until hot. Add 1 teaspoon of the butter and tilt the pan to coat the bottom with the butter as it melts. Ladle about ¼ cup (2 fl oz/60 ml) of the batter into the pan, tilting and swirling the pan to coat the bottom with the batter. Pour any excess batter back into the bowl. Cook until the edges dry and separate slightly from the pan, 30–45 seconds. Using a spatula, turn the crêpe and cook for just a few seconds. Transfer to a warmed plate and cover with aluminum foil to keep warm. Repeat with the remaining batter, adding more butter to the pan as needed. You should have about 12 crêpes.

In a frying pan over medium-high heat, melt 4 tablespoons of the Suzette Butter and add 4 crêpes to the pan. Using 2 forks, turn the crêpes in the butter to coat, then fold each into fourths and nestle them in the pan. Add 2 tablespoons of the brandy and 1 tablespoon of the Grand Marnier. Remove from the heat and using a long-handled match, ignite the brandy and stir the crêpes in the sauce until the flames subside. Transfer to individual plates. Repeat the process in 2 more batches. Serve at once, garnished with the orange zest strips.

Crêpes suzette were made famous in elegant Parisian restaurants at the turn of the twentieth century and have become standard French dessert fare. That they were accidentally created by a young waiter who was serving the Prince of Wales, and then named for the prince's companion, Suzette, is a nice story, but probably not true. Nevertheless, they are dramatic and utterly delicious.

Almond Dacquoise

Although the result is stunning, this is not a difficult cake to make. Meringue is piped into circles, then baked and layered with buttercream frosting. The meringue almost always includes nut flour; this one uses almond flour, but hazelnut (filbert), walnut, or even pistachio flour could be used instead.

To make the meringue layers, preheat the oven to 300°F (150°C). Line 3 baking sheets with parchment (baking) paper. Using the bottom of a 9-inch (23-cm) round cake pan, trace a circle onto each sheet of parchment.

In a small bowl, whisk together ²/₃ cup (5 oz/155 g) of the granulated sugar and the almond flour. In a large bowl, using an electric mixer, beat the egg whites until soft peaks form. Add 3 tablespoons of the granulated sugar and continue beating. Slowly add the remaining sugar and beat until stiff peaks form. Beat in the almond extract. Using a rubber spatula, gently fold in the almond flour mixture.

Spoon the batter into a pastry (piping) bag fitted with the ¹/₂-inch (12-mm) plain tip. Starting at the center of one of the circles on the parchment, pipe the batter in a concentric circle until you reach the edge of the circle. Repeat to pipe the mixture into the remaining parchment circles. Bake until the meringues are pale gold and firm, 1–1¹/₂ hours. Transfer them, still on the paper, to wire racks to cool.

To make the buttercream, in a bowl, whisk the egg yolks until pale yellow. In a saucepan over medium heat, combine the milk and granulated sugar and bring to a simmer. Whisk ¹/₂ cup (4 fl oz/125 ml) of the hot milk mixture into the yolks. Pour the yolk mixture into the pan and whisk just until thickened, about 3 minutes; do not overcook. Remove from the heat and whisk until slightly cooled, 3–4 minutes. Whisk in the butter and espresso powder and beat until fluffy.

To assemble the dacquoise, gently peel the cooled meringues away from the parchment. Using a serrated knife, trim the meringues so that they are the same size. Transfer a meringue to a cake plate. Using an icing spatula, spread about one-fourth of the buttercream on top. Top with another meringue and spread with about one-third of the remaining buttercream. Top with the remaining meringue layer. Spread the remaining buttercream on the top and sides of the dacquoise. Loosely cover with aluminum foil or plastic wrap and refrigerate until the buttercream is firm, at least 4 hours or up to overnight.

Let the dacquoise return to room temperature before serving. Pour the cocoa powder into a small sieve and dust the top of the cake with the cocoa powder. Using a serrated knife, cut into wedges and serve.

For the meringue layers

1 cup (8 oz/250 g) granulated sugar minus 2 tablespoons

²/₃ cup (4 oz/120 g) almond flour

5 large egg whites, at room temperature

¹/₄ teaspoon pure almond extract

¹/₈ teaspoon salt

For the buttercream frosting

4 large egg yolks

1 cup (8 fl oz/250 ml) whole milk

¹/₂ cup (4 oz/125 g) granulated sugar

1 cup (8 oz/250 g) unsalted butter, at room temperature

3 tablespoons instant espresso powder

Cocoa powder for dusting

MAKES 10 SERVINGS

AQUITAINE

Prunes in Armagnac

For the prunes

½ lemon

1 cup (8 oz/250 g) sugar

½ vanilla bean pod

1 lb (500 g) prunes

3 cups (24 fl oz/750 ml) Armagnac

Crème Chantilly (page 271) or Crème Fraîche Ice Cream (page 230), for serving

Lemon zest strips for serving, (optional)

MAKES 1 QUART (1 L);
6–8 SERVINGS

Using a sharp knife, remove the zest from the lemon half in a few large strips.

In a medium saucepan over medium-high heat, combine the sugar and 1 cup (8 fl oz/250 ml) water and bring to a boil. Add the vanilla pod and the lemon zest strips. Reduce the heat to medium-low and simmer, stirring, until the sugar dissolves, about 5 minutes. Remove from the heat, cover, and let the sugar syrup stand overnight at room temperature to let the flavors blend.

Remove the vanilla pod and lemon zest from the syrup and discard. Add the prunes and Armagnac to the sugar syrup. Transfer to a clean glass jar, cover tightly, and store in a cool, dark place for at least 2 months before serving. The prunes will keep in an airtight container at room temperature for up to 1 year.

When ready to serve, divide the prunes and syrup among 6 glass dishes. Top with a dollop of Cream Chantilly or a scoop of Crème Frâiche Ice Cream. Garnish with lemon zest strips, if using, and serve at once.

Prunes are grown in southwestern France, which is also the home of Armagnac, a brandy made by distilling a blend of white wines. A natural pairing of the two, this dessert is a marriage made in heaven. If you're feeling particularly indulgent, enjoy it with a snifter of Armagnac.

Honey Madeleines

As the inspiration for Marcel Proust's monumental work, *Remembrance of Things Past*, madeleines enjoy considerable renown. What is perhaps less well known is how easy these buttery and mouthwatering cakes are to make. You will need just a few ingredients as well as a shell-shaped madeleine mold.

Have ready 1 or more madeleine molds with a total of 18 indentations. Preheat the oven to 375°F (190°C). Using a pastry brush, coat the madeleine molds with the 1 tablespoon butter, carefully buttering every ridge. Dust with the 1 tablespoon flour, tilting the molds to coat evenly. Tap gently to remove any excess flour.

In a bowl, whisk the 1 cup flour and the baking powder; set aside.

In a large bowl, using an electric mixer on medium speed, beat together the eggs, sugar, and honey until pale yellow. Add the ³/₄ cup butter, one piece at a time, beating constantly. Beating on low speed, gradually add the dry ingredients to the egg mixture.

Spoon the batter into the prepared molds. Bake the cakes until golden, about 25 minutes. Transfer to a rack to let cool in the mold. Once the cakes are cool enough to handle, remove from the mold and serve at once.

³/₄ cup (6 oz/185 g) unsalted butter, at room temperature, cut into small pieces, plus 1 tablespoon

1 cup (5 oz/155 g) all-purpose (plain) flour, plus 1 tablespoon

1 teaspoon baking powder

3 large eggs

³/₄ cup (6 oz/180 g) sugar

3 tablespoons honey

MAKES 18 MADELEINES

Floating Islands

4 egg whites, at room temperature

½ cup (4 oz/125 g) sugar, plus ⅔ cup (5 oz/150 g)

¼ teaspoon pure vanilla extract

Crème Anglaise (page 271)

MAKES 8–10 SERVINGS

In a bowl, using an electric mixer, beat the egg whites until soft peaks form. Add the ½ cup sugar and beat until stiff peaks form. Beat in the vanilla.

Line a plate with paper towels. Fill a saucepan to within 1 inch (2.5 cm) of the top with water. Place the pan over medium-high heat and bring the water to just below a simmer. Working in batches and using 2 soup spoons, drop mounds of the egg white mixture into the water and cook for 3–4 minutes. Turn off the heat and continue to cook until the whites are firm, 5–8 minutes longer. Transfer the meringues to the paper towels to drain.

In a medium saucepan over medium heat, combine the ⅔ cup sugar and 1 tablespoon water. Cook, stirring with a wooden spoon, until the sugar dissolves. Continue to cook, without stirring, until a light caramel syrup forms, 4–8 minutes. Remove from the heat.

In a small saucepan over low heat, gently warm the Crème Anglaise.

Divide the Crème Anglaise among 8–10 shallow bowls. Using a spatula, slide 2 or 3 meringues into each bowl and drizzle with the caramel syrup. Serve at once.

Called *îles flottants*, these islands of egg whites drizzled with caramel and floating in a sea of crème anglaise are considered an old-fashioned dessert, but one that is coming back into fashion. It is easy to make at home and creates an impressive end to a meal.

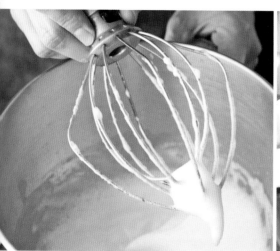

Crème Brûlée

Crème brûlée, "burnt cream," is the grown-up relative of crème caramel, both of which are found across France, even in convenience stores. Both are custards, but crème brûlée is richer and thicker and is covered with a thin layer of caramelized dark brown sugar, which cracks under your spoon as you break it.

Preheat the oven to 325°F (165°C).

Have ready four ³/₄-cup (6–fl oz/180-ml) heatproof ramekins and a shallow baking dish just large enough to hold the ramekins.

In a bowl, beat the egg yolks and the vanilla until the mixture thickens.

In a saucepan over medium-high heat, warm the cream and granulated sugar, stirring, until small bubbles form along the edges of the pan and the sugar dissolves, 3–4 minutes. Gradually whisk the cream mixture into the egg yolk mixture. Strain through a fine-mesh sieve into a bowl.

Pour the mixture into the ramekins, filling each to within ¹/₂ inch (12 mm) of the rims. Place the ramekins in the baking dish and pour boiling water into the dish until it reaches halfway up the sides of the ramekins.

Bake until the custards are set but still jiggle slightly in the middle when the ramekins are shaken, and a thin skin has formed on top, 35–40 minutes.

Transfer the baking dish to a wire rack and let the custards cool slightly. Remove the ramekins from the dish and let the custards cool to room temperature. Refrigerate until well chilled, 3–4 hours.

When ready to serve, preheat the broiler (grill). Place the brown sugar in a small sieve and, using a spoon, push it through the sieve and evenly sprinkle the tops of the custards with the sugar. Return the ramekins to the baking dish, pour cold water around them, and add several ice cubes. Broil (grill) until the brown sugar melts and caramelizes, 2–3 minutes. Alternatively, use a small kitchen torch to caramelize the sugar.

Transfer to a wire rack and let the custards cool until the surface hardens, about 10 minutes. Serve at once.

4 large egg yolks

¹/₂ teaspoon pure vanilla extract

2 cups (16 fl oz/500 ml) heavy (double) cream

¹/₄ cup (2 oz/60 g) granulated sugar

Boiling water

2 tablespoons firmly packed brown sugar

Ice cubes

MAKES 4 SERVINGS

Canelés

2¼ cups (18 fl oz/560 ml) whole milk

1 vanilla bean pod, split

2 large eggs, plus 2 large egg yolks

1¼ cups (10 oz/315 g) sugar

1 cup (5 oz/155 g) plus 2 tablespoons all-purpose (plain) flour

4 tablespoons (2 oz/60 g) unsalted butter, melted, plus 2 tablespoons unsalted butter, at room temperature

1 tablespoon light rum

Confectioners' (icing) sugar for dusting

MAKES 15–18 CAKES

Pour the milk into a saucepan. Scrape the vanilla seeds into the milk and add the pod. Warm the milk over medium-high heat until small bubbles form along the edges of the pan, about 5 minutes. Remove from the heat and set aside to cool.

In a small bowl, beat the eggs. In another bowl, beat the egg yolks.

In a large bowl, whisk together the sugar and the flour. Make a well in the center and whisk in the whole eggs followed by the egg yolks to make a thick paste. Remove the vanilla bean pod from the milk and discard. Add the warm milk, melted butter, and rum to the egg mixture and whisk until blended. Cover the batter and refrigerate for at least 1 hour or up to 2 hours.

Preheat the oven to 350°F (180°C). Coat *canelé* molds (page 40) or a 12-cup muffin pan with some of the 2 tablespoons butter and refrigerate for 15 minutes.

Remove the batter from the refrigerator and stir well. Fill each chilled mold or muffin cup almost to the rim with the batter. If using the molds, place on a rimmed baking sheet. Bake until the *canelés* are dark brown and puffed on the edges, with a slight depression in the center, about 1 hour; do not open the oven during baking. Using pot holders, unmold the *canelés* onto a wire rack while still hot.

Continue buttering, chilling, and filling the molds, and baking the *canelés* until all of the batter has been used. Refrigerate the batter between batches.

Serve warm or at room temperature with a dusting of confectioners' sugar.

These caramel cakes, a specialty of Bordeaux, have a dark brown, caramelized exterior and a moist, airy interior. The insides of the molds are greased with pure beeswax to help produce the signature dark crust, but butter works just as well. The cakes require special *canelé* molds, preferably copper, but the investment is worth the resulting unique, dainty cakes.

Pain au Chocolat

Use croissant dough to make this classic French treat, a flaky roll concealing a gooey stripe of bittersweet chocolate. Eat these pastries within a few hours of being baked to ensure that the chocolate is still soft. To save some for another day, after forming and before baking, line them on a parchment-covered tray, cover with plastic wrap, and freeze for up to 2 weeks. Let thaw in the refrigerator overnight, then let rise and bake according to the directions.

Lightly butter 2 baking sheets.

Using a box grater or a food processor, coarsely grate or chop the chocolate.

On a lightly floured work surface, roll out the dough into a 12-by-16-inch (30-by-40-cm) rectangle. Cut the dough lengthwise into 3 equal strips, then cut each strip crosswise into 4 squares, for a total of 12 squares. Working with 1 square at a time, place a rounded tablespoon of the grated chocolate in a strip in the middle of the dough. Fold the bottom up a third of the way and fold the top down so that it slightly overlaps the bottom flap. Pinch the seam to seal. Place on the baking sheet, seam side down. Repeat with the remaining dough squares and chocolate, spacing the rolls 2–3 inches (5–7.5 cm) apart. Cover loosely with a kitchen towel and let the pastries rise at room temperature until they double in bulk, about 1 1/2 hours.

Preheat the oven to 425°F (220°C). Lightly brush the tops of the rolls with the egg wash. Bake the pastries until golden brown, 15–18 minutes. Let the pastries cool in the pan on a rack. Serve warm or at room temperature. Store the baked pastries in an airtight container at room temperature for up to 1 day.

Unsalted butter for greasing

6 oz (185 g) bittersweet or semisweet (plain) chocolate

All-purpose (plain) flour for dusting

2 lb (1 kg) Croissant Dough (page 274)

1 large egg beaten with 1 tablespoon whole milk

MAKES 12 ROLLS

Les Sauces and Les Condiments

French cuisine is famous for its sauces and condiments. Tapenade, aioli, and *anchoïade* often appear with hors d'oeuvres. *Sauce nantua* and *sauce gribiche* partner well with meat and fish. Crème chantilly and crème anglaise gild desserts. Many recipes here can be made in advance.

Beurre Blanc

½ cup (3 oz/90 g) minced shallots

½ cup (4 fl oz/125 ml) white wine vinegar

½ cup (4 fl oz/125 ml) dry white wine

¼ teaspoon salt

⅛ teaspoon freshly ground white pepper

1½ cups (12 oz/375 g) cold butter, cut into small pieces

In a saucepan over medium-high heat, combine the shallots, vinegar, wine, salt, and pepper. Bring to a boil and cook until reduced to about 2 tablespoons, about 2 minutes. Remove from the heat. Add 2 or 3 pieces of the butter and beat until the sauce is creamy but still opaque. Return to very low heat, add the remaining butter, 1 piece at a time, and beat until creamy. Remove from the heat. Transfer to a warmed bowl and serve at once.

Makes 1½ cups (12 fl oz/375 ml)

Rouille

2 dried cayenne or other red chiles

4 cloves garlic

1 tablespoon dried bread crumbs

2 large egg yolks

½ teaspoon sea salt

½ cup (4 fl oz/125 ml) extra-virgin olive oil

Lay each chile flat on a cutting board. Use a small, sharp knife to slit in half lengthwise. Open each chile and spread it out on the cutting board. Cut around the stem end and remove the seeds.

In a mortar, combine the chiles and garlic. Using a pestle, and working in a circular motion, grind together until a smooth paste forms. Add the bread crumbs and crush them with the pestle. Add the egg yolks and the salt and crush with the pestle to make a smooth paste. Add the olive oil in a slow, steady stream, grinding with the pestle until the mixture thickens to the consistency of mayonnaise. Alternatively, in a blender or food processor, combine the chiles, garlic, bread crumbs, egg yolks, and salt and process until a paste forms. With the motor running, add the olive oil in a slow, steady stream, processing until the mixture is the consistency of mayonnaise. Use at once, or refrigerate in an airtight container for up to 1 week.

Makes ¾ cup (6 fl oz/180 ml)

Sauce Verte

2 slices baguette, crusts removed

¼ cup (2 fl oz/60 ml) red wine vinegar

2½ tablespoons extra-virgin olive oil

½ cup (½ oz/15 g) finely chopped fresh flat-leaf (Italian) parsley leaves

2 tablespoons capers

2 cloves garlic, minced

3 olive oil–packed anchovy fillets, minced

1 tablespoon sugar

2 tablespoons minced cornichons

Put the baguette slices in a bowl and crumble the bread with your fingers. Pour the vinegar and olive oil over the bread and let stand for

5 minutes. With a fork, stir in the parsley, capers, garlic, anchovies, sugar, and cornichons until combined; the sauce will be thick. Use at once.

Makes ¾ cup (6 fl oz/180 ml)

Sauce Nantua

1 lb (500 g) crayfish or shrimp (prawn) shells

½ cup (4 fl oz/125 g) unsalted butter, melted, plus 2 tablespoons

¼ cup (1½ oz/45 g) minced yellow onion

2 tablespoons all-purpose (plain) flour

1 cup (8 fl oz/250 ml) milk, heated

½ teaspoon kosher or sea salt

¼ teaspoon freshly ground white pepper

1 bay leaf

½ cup (4 fl oz/125 ml) heavy (double) cream

Preheat the oven to 300°F (150°C).

Spread the crayfish or shrimp shells on a baking sheet and bake until dry, but not browned, about 10 minutes. Transfer the shells to a food processor and process until finely ground. In a large saucepan over low heat, combine the ground shells, the ½ cup melted butter, and 2 tablespoons water.

Cook, stirring occasionally, and being careful not to let the butter boil, until the butter turns pink in color and is infused with shellfish flavor, about 10 minutes.

Line a fine-mesh sieve with several layers of cheesecloth (muslin) and strain the butter into a small bowl. Cover tightly and refrigerate until firm. This can be done up to 3 days in advance. In another large saucepan over medium-high heat, melt the 2 tablespoons butter. Add the onion and cook until translucent, about 2 minutes. Remove from the heat and whisk in the flour to make a roux. Return to the heat and gradually pour in the hot milk, whisking constantly